Maggie May's Diary

Maggie May's Diary

Thomas E. Coughlin

Tom Coughlin
Kennebunkport, ME

Fitzgerald & LaChapelle Publishing

Manufactured in the United States of America

Library of Congress Catalog Card Number: 98-73598

ISBN: 0-9666202-0-8

Cover design: Pearl and Associates

Book design and production: Tabby House

Second printing, August 1999

Fitzgerald & LaChapelle Publishing
852 Elm Street
Manchester, N.H. 03101
(603) 669-6112
fax (603) 641-4929

Dedication

For Mary Elizabeth Coughlin...
in return for a debt beyond repayment

1

IT WAS MID-AFTERNOON IN LATE AUGUST when Margaret Keogh-Olson left her office in Manchester and headed home to Bedford, an upper middle-class suburb on the city's southwest perimeter. It was a pleasant season in New Hampshire. The oppressive summer heat was largely over, leaving behind warm, invigorating days and cool, comfortable nights. Margaret was traveling home to scour her attic for old photographs from her high school years. She would be attending her fifteen-year reunion soon. The event's organizers had asked alumni to provide photos in advance for decoration. The photographs of many attendees would also appear in the evening's program. Margaret received word to submit all photographs by August 31 and time was growing short.

She breezed across town in moderate traffic, two hours ahead of the crush of cars that would clog the roadways by five o'clock. Her early departure from the office this day was just one benefit of self-employment. As owner of a thriving accounting practice, Margaret set all her own rules. She consulted no one if something had to be done during normal working hours. Consultation was for her employees to do through her.

When she got home, Margaret changed into an old sweatshirt and pair of shorts, then climbed the stairs to the attic of her spacious, colonial home. She knew exactly where to begin looking for her high school memorabilia. An ancient trunk in the attic was the depository for most of these remembrances. Originally, the trunk had belonged to her father. It dated back to his days in the New Hampshire National Guard. She knew instinctively that most all of her teenage collectibles would be found somewhere in that wooden crate.

Upon reaching the top of the stairs, Margaret found the trunk in the far corner of the dusty attic. Painstakingly, she began sifting through papers, photographs, rock concert ticket stubs, and adolescent souvenirs. Margaret paused as recollections attached to certain objects swept over her. She placed a set of flattering pictures from a senior-year outing next to her on the floor before continuing to rummage through the locker.

After sweeping aside piles of meaningless school papers, the corner of a vaguely familiar brown object came to light. It took a few seconds before Margaret identified what she had just uncovered—it was a diary. The sight of this remnant from her youth caught her by surprise, causing her to stare down at it almost in disbelief. In an instant Margaret remembered that it was not just any ordinary object. Within the covers of this plain, brown binder she had chronicled a large part of her sophomore year at Southside High School. Following a prolonged hesitation, she reached down and picked it up. The sunlight through the attic window was providing enough light, allowing her to read quite comfortably. Slumping back against the attic wall, Margaret flipped open the imitation-leather cover, revealing the first entry.

September 8, 1972

Dear Diary...I can already tell that this year's going to be better than last. The boys are cuter in my classes and I like the teachers more, especially Mr. Brody.

An emotional swell rose from deep within her. She had not opened this diary in more than fifteen years and this realization struck her with a thought-provoking wallop. She considered how the girl who had written these words so many years earlier now seemed distant and foreign to her. Margaret stopped and marveled at the sensation she was experiencing. She pondered over whether the diary was speaking to her or whether she was actually speaking to herself. There was only one additional entry on the first page.

September 11, 1972

Dear Diary...I have definitely found the boy that I want to ask me out. Ronald Bilodeau has the sexiest smile in the whole school and he's soooo tall. He doesn't know it but Maggie May Keogh will be laying claim to those two lips that gives us that sexy smile and real soon too. If I really hit the books in History and raise my hand to answer a lot he'll notice me. I only wish I sat closer to him.

Margaret chuckled to herself as she completed reading the entry. She was finding the diary quite amusing. She had almost forgotten that Margaret Keogh-Olson, Certified Public Accountant, was for a time, Maggie May Keogh, thanks to the popularity of a Rod Stewart single from the early seventies. Margaret paused and tried to remember the last time anyone had called her that. She recalled her mother calling her Maggie May, but that was only when her mom was needling her, and she had not thought of doing it in years. Margaret read on, skipping over some of the wordier entries.

September 18, 1972

Dear Diary...I can't believe it but there is this guy in the hallway who keeps staring at me and smiling. He's not in any of my classes and I think he may be a senior. I don't know what I'll do if he talks to me. Ronald acts like such a jerk around his friends and some of the girls who hang out with them. I really don't think anything is going to happen on that front.

Margaret sat back, amazed at how young and uncomplicated she had been. Running the math in her head, Margaret calculated she was fifteen when these entries were made. Her daughter, Jenny, was born late in the summer of 1973, meaning she was definitely fifteen. This meant that the "ordeal," as she was accustomed to calling it, would not occur for a few months. She remembered receiving definitive word of her pregnancy the following winter. Pausing momentarily, Margaret asked herself if she was prepared to read the entries from the early stages of the pregnancy. She opted for putting this off. Instead, she decided to scan ahead to a few pages covering the early weeks of the school year.

October 2, 1972

Dear Diary...I had great hopes for this year just a few weeks ago. What's happening? I'm sitting with the same people at lunch as I did my freshman year. Even Mr. Brody's class is boring. Will anything exciting ever happen to me?

October 3, 1972

Dear Diary...Maggie May took some initiative and talked to 3 cute boys today...Todd Lemay, Kevin Bauer and Skip Emerson. They all spoke back and Skip even asked me about my classes and what school I went to before I came to Southside. Skip is definitely the cutest of the 3 and he may even have his license. I know he's at least 16 because he's a junior.

Margaret thumbed forward again, skimming the entries. Then, a name caught her eye. The name was Brian.

October 17, 1972

Dear Diary...Skip made a point of walking me to History class today. I'm positive he went out of his way to do it. He told me his fourth period class was on the second floor. Maggie May Keogh, you've got it! I lost the empty seat next to me in homeroom today. This tall guy who looks like he could use a bath transferred to our school and lucky me he gets the empty desk next to mine. I liked having that desk empty to use as my personal table for my stuff. Now if this guy looked a little more like Rod Stewart who is also tall and thin there wouldn't be a problem. I'm not sure if it's his wrinkled clothes or the fact that he might try shaving his face once in a while but he looks like one of those tough guys from shop class or that hangs out downtown after school. His name is Brian Kiley or Kelly or maybe it's just Kreepy with a "K." I caught him looking over at me this afternoon. This is one conquest I can do without.

October 18, 1972

Dear Diary...I barely spoke to Skip today. He waved to me in the hall...big deal. I know he still thinks I'm cute. All of a sudden I have Brian Kelly everywhere I look. He's in my English class now. I thought he was going to talk to me in homeroom this morning. Oh please, God, I'm not ready to deal with someone like that now. I think I'll be nice and friendly with Skip tomorrow. That's it Maggie May, be bubbly.

Margaret put down the diary for a moment as a new wave of memories washed over her. Brian Kelly was someone she had intentionally pushed to the back of her mind. There were too many bittersweet emotions waiting to be stirred up. She still retained a smattering of guilt from her association with this boy, even after all these years. There was no question, Brian Kelly had left his mark on her personal history. Margaret's rational side told her to put the diary back in the footlocker, but she was hooked on her own personal melodrama by now. She would read on. Again, she thumbed forward a few pages to speed the process.

November 10, 1972

Dear Diary...Brian Kelly is so strange. I never should have started talking to him. I wish there was some way to just back away from this situation and go back to not knowing each other. Skip saw me talking to Brian today and didn't like it. In English class Brian told Ben Turner to go fuck himself. Ben had just been kidding around and making cracks about how Brian wears the same clothes over and over and Brian tells him to go fuck himself in this real loud voice. I didn't think any of the boys had the guts to say that to Ben's face. Everyone screamed for Ben to punch out Brian but he didn't. He said he wasn't going to let some low life get him kicked out of school and off the football team for fighting but I think it may have been more than that. Brian looks really poor and the poor kids are tougher than the other ones. I don't think Ben knew what to expect from Brian and so no fight. Well now no one is speaking to Brian because Ben's real popular and all. God I wish I hadn't started talking to Brian.

November 13, 1972

Dear Diary...Skip is now sitting with me at lunch. It is sooo nice. Things are going real good with Skip and Brian was absent from school today. Skip is coming over to visit this weekend. This will be the first time I've spent any time with him away from school.

P.S. There is one problem. Skip doesn't like Rod Stewart and calls him a fag. I'll have to work on that.

November 20, 1972

Dear Diary...Skip came to the house on Saturday and spent the afternoon with me. Cindy and Gayle are so jealous because he drives and his parents let him use their car. We saw "The Heartbreak Kid" at the Bedford Mall and it was really funny. Sitting in the theater with Skip was sooo romantic. I am so incredibly happy.

November 21, 1972

Dear Diary...Brian was finally back in school today. I am probably the only kid in school, well the only girl, who talks to him. He is a lot more intelligent than a lot of people think. He said he got an A- in English last term. He asked me if I would like to read his composition in English and maybe he could read mine. Oh God, how do I get this guy off my case? I really think Brian is a nice guy and all but if he screws up things with Skip I'll kill him. I wish I could be more like Cindy sometimes and just shoot boys down.

Lowering the diary to her lap, Margaret stared dreamily across the attic floor. How many times over the years had she thought back to that slumber party and run all the "what if" questions through her mind? What if Cindy's parents had decided not to go to Connecticut that weekend? What if Skip had not been able to get out that night? What if things had not gone as far as they had? What if she had not become pregnant?

Margaret was aware that in the next few pages there would be much written about that night at Cindy's. She and Gayle put together the plan of action, setting up all the details of their romantic evening. Margaret was surprised to realize that she was eager to relive the orchestration of this common schoolgirl prank.

First though, she picked herself up from the dusty, wooden floorboards, and descended two flights of stairs to the first floor of the house. After pouring herself a glass of white wine, she curled up on the couch and leafed forward in the journal to beyond Thanksgiving Day. She remembered that the beginning of the planning process for the overnight at Cindy's began just after the long Thanksgiving weekend.

December 4, 1972

Dear Diary...I have finally, I think, convinced Skip that Brian is nothing more than a friend and that there is nothing even close to a romance involved. This is really good because I know Skip is afraid to say anything to Brian about not talking to me. Brian seems to have gotten the message that I don't think of him in a romantic way. Cindy was saying today that her parents are going out of town sometime before Christmas and she is trying to convince them to let her stay behind. Now if she can talk her parents into letting her stay home then maybe Gayle and I can stay with her. Now if that is possible then maybe Skip and the guys could also come by for a while and we could get some Boone's Farm Wine and put together a really romantic evening. By the way diary...I really don't think this can work because too many things can go wrong. But it really makes a great dream.

December 5, 1972

Dear Diary...Brian got in real trouble today. Ben Turner tried to show him up by pushing his head down when he reached for something on the floor. Brian came up swinging and hit Ben at least a couple of times when Miss Royal came back into the class. She sent Brian to the main office and he got two demerits for fighting. Everyone thought it was a big joke. Brian said something to Ben about catching him alone when his football faggots weren't around to help him. I should have said something to Miss Royal after class but I didn't. I don't think Brian expected me to do or say something. When I talked to Brian in homeroom before leaving he never said anything about being mad at me. He said the two demerits would keep him off the honor roll for sure. I couldn't tell if he was kidding or not. Maybe I should've said something.

December 6, 1972

Dear Diary...Cindy's parents are going to let her stay home next weekend. I can't believe it! Now I've got to decide whether to tell Mom and Dad about being alone next Friday at Cindy's or take a chance they won't call Cindy's parents. It's probably best to be up front with them and hope for the best. Then there's the problem of whether Skip can make it over that night.

December 7, 1972

Dear Diary...Mom and Dad say it's OK to spend the night at Cindy's. I know Mom half suspects something involving boys because of all the trust and confidence speeches she is laying on me. I really hate to have to do all this sort of stuff and lying and all but I think it's the only way at this point. At least I was honest about Cindy being alone in the house. Gayle told her parents that it was just a pajama party. Tomorrow I ask Skip. It is all going too smoothly.

December 8, 1972

Dear Diary...Skip says he can definitely make it next Friday but not all night. That's OK. I keep getting this feeling that something is going to screw this night up. Everything has just gone too well. Gayle opened her big mouth in front of Brian today about next Friday and now I'm getting 20 questions from him. I told him it was personal and if I wanted to share it with him I would. Then I told him that if he valued our friendship he'd just drop it, and he did. I have this feeling of power when I deal with Brian. I know he still really likes me and I have the upper hand on him. Cindy and Gayle tease me about how he acts around me. I think he probably thinks about me in bed at night before he goes to sleep. Everyone thinks like that but I bet I'm the one he thinks about. If I asked him he'd probably say it was Raquel

Welch or someone like that. Oh, one last thing, Brian told me he has really started to get into Rod Stewart lately. That is soooo pitiful. I really shouldn't laugh at him. He is a pretty nice guy.

Margaret shuffled a page or two, scanning the entries until she spotted her writing from the day after the overnight at Cindy's. She was curious to see if her first reaction to that evening bore any similarity to the memory she constructed in her mind over the years.

December 16, 1972

Dear Diary...I am now a woman. I have lost my innocence. I am a woman of the world. Be serious Maggie May. Skip and I made love last night in Cindy's bedroom. It was the first time for me and I think it was Skip's first time too in spite of what he says. God, I wish I could say how the earth moved and I was lifted to heights of ecstasy never even dreamed of before. The truth is it hurt and was really awkward. I was nervous but I think Skip was even more nervous. This is really weird but after we were done and the guys had left and Gayle and Cindy had gone to bed I had a hard time going to sleep. I kept thinking about that record the radio stations used to play a couple of years ago...Is That All There Is?...by that old singer Patty Page or Peggy Lee or somebody. I always hated it when the DJ would play that song. Is there something wrong with me? It was over so fast and while it was happening I could only think about how much it hurt. Maybe Skip wasn't doing it right? Is this why some girls talk about doing it with older guys in their twenties...because they have experience and know exactly how to do it? This is heavy stuff! One thing's for sure. I will definitely have to start hiding my diary a little better after this. Oh God, I can just picture Dad reading this. Oh my God.

Margaret looked up from the journal and considered her words from many years before. A smile creased above her mouth. She was looking at herself in the second person. She read almost in disbelief, marveling at her own innocence. There was no mention of protection or pregnancy. The young Margaret Keogh expressed no concern over whether Skip would bring word of his conquest to school. A major event with far-reaching consequences had taken place in her life, and Maggie May had not the remotest clue of it.

Her mind danced with idle thoughts of the overnight before a question surfaced: Did she really want to relive that period of anguish leading up to the word from Doctor Aronberg? Did she want to relive the day of the eventful news? Why not just close the diary and go back to her original business, finding the photographs from her senior year? Following some internal debate, Margaret read a small sampling from the entries in January.

> *January 5, 1973*
>
> *Dear Diary...I can't think of anything anymore but when is my period going to come? I'm at least 5 or 6 days late and the pressure is killing me. I can't study and I keep breaking out in crying fits when I'm alone. I have to talk to someone. Brian's noticed the change and he keeps asking if I want to talk. Skip seems to be mad at me over everything but he still doesn't know what I'm going through. I made a vow to Jesus today that if I come through this without being pregnant I will not do it again until I'm married. Now it's even in writing. Please Jesus, don't let this happen to me.*

Margaret closed the journal as a rush of discomfort came over her. Maggie May Keogh had been a child when the school year started. However, a transformation took place as the days of her sophomore year played out. The following pages of the diary chronicled a large part of her maturing process—the difficult days leading up to word of her pregnancy. Still, Margaret was caught up in this story, written by her own hand. Nevertheless, there would also be precious moments she found herself wanting to relive. Margaret hoped to minimize the painful memories from that period. Hence, she decided to scan the pages and read only entries where Brian Kelly's name appeared.

The diary was allowing Margaret to mentally time-travel back to her youth. She envisioned brain cells awakening in a deep recess of her mind. Minute and subtle details from her teen years were coming back to her. Foremost among her recollections were the memories of her friendship with Brian Kelly. Unquestionably there would be much in the way of personal heartache chronicled in this journal over the next few months.

> *March 14, 1973*
>
> *Dear Diary...It is starting to become pretty clear to me that the word is out. I know I'm still not showing yet but I keep catching kids in the hall looking at me and laughing. Skip swears he hasn't said anything to anybody but I don't believe him. I know Brian wouldn't say anything to anyone. Of course, there is Cindy. I know she suspects something but I really can't ask her anything because then she would*

know for sure. God I hate this. I keep finding myself standing alone in the hall or sitting by myself in the library or lunch room. Today I was standing in the hall waiting for the next bell and really feeling alone when two hands come down on my shoulders from behind. When I turned it was Brian and he just smiled. He said I had to stop daydreaming about him all day and get cracking with the books. Driving home from school today I realized that Brian is my best friend.

March 21, 1973

Dear Diary...Cindy took me aside today and told me that the word was out. She said that she thought that I would want to know and that it should come from a friend. I wanted to tell her that she hasn't been much of a friend lately but I didn't have the nerve. I thought I heard the first wisecrack about the baby today but I made believe I didn't hear it. Brian made the honor roll this term. He warned me not to start sucking up to him now that the world knew he was a genius.

March 22, 1973

Dear Diary...I gave Brian a congratulations card about making the honor roll. It was one of those joke cards. It said congratulations but warned him that if you took away his great intellect, tremendous good looks, family fortune, creative genius, and charismatic personality, he'd be a nothing like the rest of us. I left it in his desk in the morning and when he found it and read it I thought he was going to start crying or something. He made such a big deal of it.

March 23, 1973

Dear Diary...I wish I could just quit school and stay home until the baby comes. I've never been more humiliated before in my life. A fat, pregnant woman was walking by the school just before Spanish class today and Gloria Sims points at her and says in a real loud voice. "Hey Keogh, there you go in three months." A couple of people in class told her to shut up but a lot just laughed. I was so humiliated I nearly started to cry. I didn't know what to do. I just sat there. Mrs. Regan came in right away and told everyone to quiet down but I don't think she heard what was said. Brian's friend Rory is in the class so Brian found out about it. He called me at home tonight and we talked for almost an hour. Good old Brian.

Her mood saddened, reacting to these last journal entries. The youthful exuberance exhibited by Maggie May in September was no longer present in her writing. That was obvious.

Margaret felt that she had read enough. However, she was curious to read the final entry in the diary. She found it a dozen pages later.

May 18, 1973

Dear Diary...Brian walked me to Mom's car again today. He whispered in my ear that he loved me.

2

MARGARET PUT DOWN THE DIARY as more details from the spring and summer of 1973 sprang from the back hallways of her memory. The house was still, allowing her to focus on those recollections unclouded by the passage of time. In spite of her parents ongoing support throughout that period, their roles in her life had become a blurred memory. Thinking back, there were only isolated incidents involving her parents that she could recall. Her mom and dad had just been there, day in and day out.

Apart from her parents, there had been no one else in her life but Brian Kelly. Brian had worked that summer at Howdy Beefburgers. She seemed to recall that much of his paycheck went to his mother. But once a week, Brian borrowed his friend Rory's car, a gaudy, green, Ford Pinto, and took her out to lunch or for a ride in the country. On two occasions he had taken her to the beach. Margaret distinctly remembered looking forward to those Tuesdays when Brian came by the house and took her somewhere—anywhere. The summer had been long and drawn out. Margaret spent the better part of every day just lying around the house in the heat and humidity. Embarrassed and self-conscious, she avoided everyone outside the family, everyone except Brian Kelly.

She vividly remembered a particular Tuesday morning. Brian was supposed to pick her up at eight o'clock. They were going to make a day of it, but Brian had remained quite secretive about their destination. It was late July and Margaret was really showing by this time. She had looked forward to this day since before the weekend. She desperately needed to get out of the house and break the monotony. Suddenly though, the clock read 8:15 then 8:30, and there was no Brian. He was always very prompt, and now he was not there. Margaret remembered returning to her room at some point and weeping in private. She had pictured Brian with a girl from work—a slim, pretty girl, not a fat, pregnant one. Margaret recalled becoming ill from disappointment as she lay across her bed, sobbing into her pillow. Somehow she never heard the car pull into the driveway. To this day Margaret could not forget the inflection in her mother's voice as she announced Brian's arrival from the front door. The expression of relief in Mrs. Keogh's tone of voice told Margaret that she had not suffered alone.

Margaret walked to the car in silence that morning, showing her irritation at Brian's tardiness. Brian ran around the gaudy, green compact and assisted her into the vehicle. He returned to the driver's seat sporting a sheepish grin.

"And how is my Maggie May on this beautiful Tuesday morning?" he asked in his usual effervescent manner.

"I began to think that you weren't going to show up," she responded bluntly.

"Well, I've got to be totally honest. When it got to be 8:30 and Raquel Welch still hadn't returned my call, I went to my list and there was Maggie May Keogh in the number two position. So here I am," he wisecracked.

"Listen Maggie, Rory had to work in Nashua today and had no way to get there without his car, so I drove him to work—and that's why I'm a little late. After all, it is Rory's car!"

"All you had to do is call and let me know, that's all," she snapped.

"You better be careful my little, stuck up girl. It almost sounds like you're becoming a little too attached to a certain semi-handsome, marginally intelligent, ruddy complexioned Irishman with grimy—"

"Enough! Drive us somewhere," Margaret exploded, unable to hide her amusement or relief.

They drove and talked for an extended time. Eventually they reached the state of Maine. Brian opened up more than usual on this day, telling her stories from his past. He spoke of his home life with his mother, and how the two of them had moved up from Lowell, Massachusetts, to Manchester, New Hampshire. He confided in her the details of personal matters, including stories of financial woes at home.

At some point during the ride Brian informed Margaret that they were going to a place his uncle had visited on vacation the previous year. His uncle had taken home movies during his stay, which Brian and his mom had seen while visiting in Massachusetts over the holidays. The place was called Parson's Beach, and it was near Wells and

Kennebunk, Maine. Brian stated repeatedly that it was one of the most beautiful beaches he had ever seen, even though it was only on the wall of his uncle's living room. Brian wanted Margaret with him on that day as he visited Parson's Beach for the first time.

Brian formed a closeness with her on this warm, July day. He confided that he had put aside almost enough money to buy a car. He spoke of bringing his mother up to Maine to see Parson's Beach, even if it took him until winter. They drove along Route 1, occasionally catching a glimpse of the ocean as they motored northward. The morning passed effortlessly as they learned more about one another. Margaret remembered that every few minutes Brian would glance down at his map. At one point he pulled completely off the road to study it. In the parking lot of a Howard Johnson's restaurant, Brian asked her if she knew what town they were in. She had guessed that they were in Wells.

"We'll be taking a right turn off Route 1 a short way ahead if you're right, and then we'll just have to watch for a sign or something," he said.

Eventually, they left Route 1 and headed toward Kennebunkport. The Pinto crawled along until they spotted a small sign indicating the road leading to Parson's Beach. Following a right turn they slowly drove toward the horizon. The roadway was lined with identically sized and spaced trees, giving the effect of a foliage arcade. Neither of them said a word, choosing to simply take in the sight of this ethereal location. After perhaps a quarter of a mile, they drew closer to the ocean. The car's tires rolled noisily over a small bridge. The ocean was not more than a hundred yards away. The beach had only a small parking lot but, as if on cue, a car pulled out and they had their parking space.

Alone in the still of her living room, Margaret thought how strange it was that certain details and impressions had stayed with her after all these years. Brian had escorted her from the car and led her to the beach over a sandy rise covered with long, dry grass. Margaret remembered thinking to herself at the time that she had just passed over a sand dune. All of her life she had heard the term "sand dune," but had never completely comprehended what it was. Now, having just walked over this small rise consisting of sand and grass, she intuitively knew she had seen her first dune. She had not said anything to Brian at the time, fearing he would laugh at her.

Having reached the shoreline, Brian suggested that they walk for a while and find a place where the crowd was less dense. Margaret reasoned that Brian was probably uncomfortable escorting a very pregnant girl in public. They strolled leisurely southward toward a rocky point down the coast. An impressive beach house stood in the distance on the rocks before them. Brian continued to speak on topics both personal and intimate: his home life, career goals, family finances, and the obstacles he knew he would face attempting to enter college in two years. Margaret was flattered that he was confiding so many previously guarded secrets in her.

They strolled along the sand for twenty minutes and were only fifty yards from the rocky point when Margaret needed to rest for a moment. She located a flat rock that slightly resembled a chair and deposited herself on it. Brian was agreeable, sensing Margaret could use a breather. She removed her sneakers and began splashing her feet in a tidal pool next to the rock. The water felt warm on her feet, and the splashing seemed to mesmerize Brian. After an extended period of silence, he spoke.

"Hey Maggie, you have really pretty feet, and don't take this compliment lightly. A lot of girls, and just about all guys have ugly feet—because of wearing shoes that are too tight and due to evolution. I think evolution is taking away one of our toes, probably the little one." Brian spoke playfully, letting her know he was only trying to have a little fun with her. However, his words had struck a nerve.

"If you think I have pretty feet now, when they're all swollen up from the baby, then come back after it's born and they're back to normal, then you'll see pretty feet." Margaret remembered she had spoken with genuine intensity. Brian could only stare at her for the next few seconds, a dumbfounded expression covering his face. Moments later, a wide grin replaced the look of surprise.

"Now there's the little egomaniac that caught my eye back at Southside High. I do believe that Maggie May, the heartbreaker, is not dead after all. Good for you." His last words came in a half whisper. Margaret reached out to him that moment for a hug. He joined her on the rock, embracing her with one arm. Nothing was said for the next few minutes. They just sat, watching and listening to the crashing waves.

As Margaret continued to draw upon her recollections, she recalled that Brian asked her pointedly about her plans following the baby's birth. He was quite direct with his inquiry. She told him that after the baby was born, her parents would assume a large part of the responsibility for raising the baby. Margaret confided in Brian that her mom and dad would raise the baby until she completed her education. What Margaret did not tell Brian was that her plans did not include returning to Southside High. Instead, she would attend a parochial school, Bishop Croteau High, located about fifteen miles from Manchester. Her parents had concluded that if she was to resume leading a normal teenage life, a fresh start was an important first step. Margaret did not disclose this to Brian, knowing it would trouble him.

Before leaving the rock that day, Brian again told Margaret that he loved her. She remembered the sincerity on his face and in his voice as he awkwardly spoke the words.

They made a pledge that day, a pledge never to allow themselves to drift apart. Margaret remembered toying with the idea of telling Brian that she loved him, too. Perhaps it was to lift his spirits, or maybe just to see the look on his face. In the end, she had decided against it. That Tuesday spent with Brian Kelly at Parson's Beach proved to be the highlight of Margaret Keogh's social life in the summer of 1973.

Thinking of Brian Kelly through the years had always churned up a heartsick feeling in her. This day was no exception. Margaret reminded herself that she had never encouraged his affection, but in spite of this, there had always been a lingering guilt associated with anything concerning Brian. She had held back much of herself from him and never fully understood the reason for it. The images from Parson's Beach slowly blurred in her mind as the events from 1973 sped forward through her awakened memory.

* * *

Jenny Keogh was born on September 11, 1973. Scores of relatives crowded Margaret's room throughout her three-day stay at the Elliot Hospital in Manchester. Brian visited mother and daughter in the hospital the following few days.

She remembered that he spent a large part of his time backed against the far wall, elbowed aside by doting aunts and cousins. Margaret thought that she may have unintentionally hurt Brian's feelings during his visits by not paying much attention to him. In truth, the baby and a sea of relatives proved to be extremely distracting.

Two weeks after giving birth, Margaret began attending Bishop Croteau High School while her parents helped care for the baby. She made friends quickly. Margaret decided to make up for lost time and Bishop Croteau High gave her the opportunity to do it. Although not a Roman Catholic, Margaret was well suited to the more structured setting of a parochial school. She got involved in school activities and modified her personality. She became a little more zany and carefree. In the end, Margaret Keogh emerged a more popular girl than the immature one who had attended Southside High.

Gradually, Margaret and Brian drifted apart. In retrospect, she thought it was essentially her fault. They went to a couple of movies together after Jenny was born, but they found themselves traveling in different circles. Their schedules became incompatible. Sometime in October Margaret told Brian that getting together was becoming too difficult. Margaret suggested that they should remain in touch by phone. At the time she knew she was bringing the friendship to an end and Brian did, too. But she no longer had the time or the desire to keep the relationship afloat. Their friendship had become an inconvenience to her. To go anywhere, they would have to use her car. Brian was not able to buy the car from his savings over the summer. A financial crisis at home had required his help. Moreover, Brian had nothing in common with Margaret's new friends from school. After a painful telephone conversation, when she suggested that they stay in touch by phone, Margaret only spoke to Brian on one more occasion.

One evening a couple of months later, Margaret was excited to attend a Christmas party with her friends. Her coat was already on, and the three classmates who had come by to pick her up were clowning under a sprig of mistletoe in the hall when the phone rang. Margaret's mother answered it and called to her, indicating it was Brian Kelly. Margaret thought to herself at the time that he could not have picked a worse time to call. Thinking back, she thought she may have sounded agitated as she reached the telephone. Brian began by telling her that he really needed to speak with her and asked if there was any way he could see her. His voice sounded strained and pressured. Margaret had not spoken two words when her friends swarmed around her, hollering into the phone. She quickly realized there was no way they were going to have a conversation under the circumstances. Hurriedly, Margaret told Brian she was in a rush, but would call him back the next day.

Mrs. Keogh was in the habit of waiting up for Margaret on nights when her daughter partied or dated. Arriving home, Margaret explained to her mother that she felt guilty about the abrupt manner in which she dismissed Brian earlier in the evening. Margaret thought she detected a downhearted tone in his voice. Mrs. Keogh was quick to add that there was a good chance that Brian still felt something for Margaret, and the holidays had a way of intensifying these feelings. She theorized that Brian Kelly was probably having a bout with the holiday blues. Margaret went to bed with feelings of guilt that night. The brief conversation earlier in the evening was the last time she ever spoke to Brian Kelly, however. The next day, one thing after another came up, and she continued to delay returning his phone call. In the end, the call was never made and Margaret never heard from Brian Kelly again.

* * *

Margaret began to emerge from the trancelike state that had enveloped her. The diary had catapulted her back into the past and she was now returning to the present. She rose from the couch and brought her empty glass to the kitchen. Margaret realized she had lost complete track of time. She was acutely aware that the memory of Brian Kelly was having an unsettling effect on her. The uncovering of the diary and the reliving of these episodes from her youth were disturbing her. She realized she had a desire to find out where Brian Kelly was, and how he was doing. She questioned herself. Was she still feeling guilty over what happened so many years before? Should she take steps toward finding Brian? What if she could locate Brian Kelly after all these years? Would he think she was out of her mind if she contacted him?

She glanced up at the kitchen clock. It was a few minutes past seven. Brad was on a business trip in Atlanta, and Jenny would not be home until after nine. On a whim, she opened the phone book to the listings for Kelly's and scanned down the column. There were two Brian Kellys listed, but neither was her Brian. The middle initials of these two Brian Kellys did not match. She knew this because Brian had made jokes on a number of occasions about his middle name, and kept it a secret for a time. He would only admit that his middle initial was "C." But Margaret wore him down one day. She caught him in a moment of weakness and found out his middle name was Cornelius. Brian had been named after a distant uncle that he had hardly known.

Margaret was beginning to question the rationality of the whole idea of locating Brian when a thought came to her—Rory O'Shea. He had been Brian's closest friend at Southside. Was there a chance that Rory still lived in the area, and perhaps maintained contact with Brian? Margaret reached down for the telephone book and fanned through the pages to the "O's." Rory O'Shea, Route 102, Derry. It seemed she might be in luck. It had to be the same Rory O'Shea, she thought. It was not a common name. Margaret felt her heart begin to beat a little faster as she reached for the phone. Did she really want to do this? Rory might think she was totally mad! Margaret asked herself if she had the nerve to really do this, and simultaneously—why?

She dialed the number and nervously waited as the phone rang three times.

"Hello," said a shy, girlish voice at the other end.

"Hi, is Rory O'Shea home?" Margaret asked tentatively.

"Daddy, it's for you," called out the little girl.

The telephone was placed down on its side by the child, and Margaret heard a scurry of activity in the background before the sound of footsteps approached the phone.

"Hello," said a pleasant, male voice with a vaguely familiar ring.

"Hi, Rory. Here comes a name from the past—it's Margaret Keogh from Southside High. Do you remember me?"

"Maggie, why of course I do. How have you been? Boy, this is a surprise. What on earth can I do for you?"

By now, Margaret was really beginning to feel self-conscious about asking Rory for any information on Brian Kelly. However, there was no turning back now. She had to say something. Margaret took a deep breath and continued directly to the point.

"Well, to be totally honest Rory, I was calling to see if you could give me some information on the whereabouts of Brian Kelly. It's been ages since we last spoke, and I hoped you might have a clue to where he was living."

"Wow, you got me there," came back Rory. "After he moved away it was like he fell off the face of the earth. To be honest, I haven't spoken to, or even heard of Brian since our junior year in school. Has it been that long for you too?"

"Well, as you probably remember, we drifted apart after the baby was born, so I think I lost track of him well before you. Do you have any idea where he moved to from Manchester?" she asked.

"There's not much to tell you. We hung around together at the start of our junior year at Southside, and then after his mom died he just...."

"Wait a minute! What did you say? Brian's mother died?" Margaret blurted out.

"Yeah, you didn't know? Oh man—it was brutal! Brian was a wreck. I'll never forget it. It was right before Christmas, and I remember going from my Christmas shopping and tree decorating to changing my clothes and sitting with Brian at the funeral home. I actually felt guilty that year celebrating Christmas, while Brian was coming apart. I didn't know what to say, Maggie, or how to talk to him. He never came back to school after Christmas break. I saw him once more before he moved. He dropped in to say good-bye. He said he'd stay in touch, but you know how that is—people say it, but they never follow through. Come to think of it, he may have said he was going to live with a relative in Massachusetts."

Rory was aware of an extended period of silence from Margaret's end of the line. He apologized for not being able to help her more.

Margaret thanked him for his help. After giving him her home phone number, Margaret asked Rory to let her know if he should ever stumble onto any information concerning Brian's whereabouts. The phone call ended, Margaret sat and reflected on the conversation. As an afterthought, Margaret considered it curious that Rory never asked why she was trying to locate Brian.

Word of Mrs. Kelly's death hung over Margaret as she walked across the kitchen floor. Brian's mother was his only real parent, and Margaret remembered they were very close. She again thought through the events in her mind of that Christmas season from seventeen years ago. An uncomfortable feeling began forming in her stomach. The last time she spoke to Brian was the evening he called as she prepared to leave the house with her friends—to attend a Christmas party. She considered a possibility. Had Brian called her about his mother? Had his mother already been ill? Had she already passed away? Had Brian needed her? Why hadn't he called back the next day?

Margaret poured herself a second glass of wine. She ran the details of Rory's conversation, and the abbreviated phone call from Brian so many years earlier, over and over in her mind. She had not been cold or rude to him, and she had intended to call him back. Margaret tried to ease the guilty feeling sweeping over her by rationalizing that she was only a kid at the time. The reality was that she had taken the easy way out. Margaret stepped back into living room and settled in a chair as the house began to grow dark. Her thoughts were only of Brian Kelly, and what a special friend he was during the most difficult period in her life. She wondered if Brian had grown to hate her after this whole affair. Brian had loved her back then, not an adult love, but a love that was blind and consuming. She thought of the people at school who had laughed at him behind his back for hanging around with the pregnant girl. Margaret remembered overhearing jokes made at his expense. She wondered if he had heard them, too.

Brian Kelly had given her everything he had, when almost everyone else had written her off as a social casualty. Then, after she decided that the relationship should be brought to an end, he had turned to her a final time. He had needed her, perhaps for just a day or two, to be there for support when he had lost his mother. Margaret tried imagining what went through his mind when she did not return his call.

Margaret knew it was ridiculous, but she began thinking of the way Brian felt about her and the way he acted in her presence. Then, she considered some of the jerks she dated later. Margaret asked herself why she had dismissed Brian so quickly? Was she too young to realize what someone like him had to offer? Was it physical? Was it socioeconomic? And what of her marriage to Brad? There was no question she and Brad were in love, but it was more of a comfortable love than a consuming love. It was more of a grown-up love than storybook. Margaret knew she would be a total malcontent if she saw others in her circle of friends consumed in their marriages. But it was not like that at all. Margaret saw her and Brad's relationship as the norm. In truth, Margaret knew she never felt as strongly toward anyone as Brian appeared to have felt toward her.

Margaret knew an unresolved matter remained regarding Brian Kelly. He had stood by her during the most traumatic period in her life, but to her amazement, Margaret could not remember if she had ever thanked him. Again, she tried rationalizing his actions. They were prompted solely due to his passionate feelings for her. This rationalization was having no effect on her guilty emotions. Margaret thought back on the many occasions when Brian expressed his love for her with such sincerity and frankness that she had felt embarrassed for him, sometimes begging him to stop. Brian had only continued, explaining that he needed to release certain pent up emotions for fear of going insane. At this moment, while sitting alone in her living room, Margaret resolved to herself that she would find Brian Kelly, no matter what. If it should take six months or a year, so be it! She would find a way. Then she was struck by a question. She did not know if Brian Kelly was even alive! Brian would be about her age—thirty-three or thirty-four, so in all probability he was. He moved back to Massachusetts. He probably moved in with his uncle. She could start looking back in Massachusetts.

Staring blankly across her living room, Margaret considered how people seemed to drift in and out of each other's lives. One day someone is working in the office next to you and at lunch you are sharing a few personal matters with them. A few weeks pass and now you are discussing harmless fantasies about who you would have an affair with under the right circumstances. Before long, you're baring your soul about someone from your past whom you could never completely forget. Sometimes you might just talk about the aspiration you carried through college that the real world has downgraded to a foolish daydream. Six months go by and your gal pal in the next office moves out of state, and you know you will never stay in touch. Family, friendships, jobs—there are no constants. Nothing seems to last!

At this moment Margaret was processing her thoughts on a different plane. The diary had jolted her emotionally. Her mind was not functioning on automatic pilot. Margaret realized she was in touch with her feelings for the first time in recent memory and she was enjoying the sensation. She decided to add her intent to find Brian Kelly to her list of formal, written goals. She knew that Brian had every right to dismiss her if she did find him, but she would not let that deter her. Margaret wanted to tell him how much his friendship had meant to her, and ask him to forgive her for what happened so many Christmas's ago. Margaret also wanted to tell Brian Kelly that she had missed him.

Suddenly, the headlights from a station wagon beamed through the front windows, and Margaret heard Jenny thanking a friend for the ride home. In a matter of seconds her daughter would be bounding through the front door and calling for her. She scooped up the diary and climbed the stairs to the second floor. Upon reaching her bedroom, she placed the diary in the top drawer of her night table by the bed. She would keep the precious journal within easy reach. Margaret knew there was no telling when the urge to spend some time with Maggie May Keogh might reappear.

3

OVER THE FOLLOWING MONTHS, Margaret's desire to locate and contact Brian Kelly dropped lower on her priority list, replaced by more mundane but more immediate concerns. In spite of the recession that gripped the country, particularly New England, her accounting and tax practice was experiencing exponential growth. She addressed the need for more office space by purchasing a building in downtown Manchester, New Hampshire. While other accounting firms in the city were downsizing, Margaret was cautiously adding staff members. The little free time she was able to set aside was spent with her daughter. Jenny was a senior in high school and Margaret knew her daughter's days living at home were numbered. Fortunately, Brad's job as an engineering consultant kept him on the road a great deal, so she avoided the conflict of juggling time between her daughter and her husband. This is not to say that the memory of Brian Kelly simply faded away. In fact, Margaret spent the better part of an afternoon that September at the Manchester City Library searching for Brian C. Kelly in numerous city phone books. A few calls were made but with no success. The diary that awakened so many feelings the summer before was now standard reading for Margaret on nights when falling asleep proved difficult.

In December 1990 Margaret hosted a Christmas party at her home in Bedford for her clients and a few close friends. This was her first major undertaking of this nature and she was determined that it would be a success. She started by booking a special musical group eight months in advance. Margaret and Brad had attended a wedding reception the previous winter at which the Pulsating Beats performed. The group impressed Margaret so much at the time that she went out of her way to approach them at the reception and inquired into their future availability. She was convinced that the group's musical ability and comical interplay with a live audience all but assured a successful party. Margaret was not the type of person to leave anything to chance.

Upon arrival, Margaret's guests were treated to the sound of smooth dinner music echoing in from her spacious living room. The mellow musical style of the Pulsating Beats was accompanied by the sight of a lavish buffet laid out on a horseshoe-shaped table in the adjoining dining room. Then, to complement the impressive spread of food in the dining room, guests were treated to the well-stocked open bar which occupied more than half of Margaret's roomy kitchen. Extra tables and chairs were scattered throughout the downstairs. Jenny Keogh and her friend Trudy Abrams roamed from room to room, serving as waitresses for the affair, while Margaret greeted each and every guest in the front hallway. Margaret had totally nailed down the logistics for a well-run party. The plan was to allow the guests about an hour and a half to finish their meals, introduce one to another, and let the alcohol generally loosen things up.

After the break that followed dinner, the Pulsating Beats returned to the gathering. The group had changed wardrobe, replacing their formal clothes with more provocative outfits. Now the entertainers took almost complete control of the party. Margaret watched with total approval as the lead singer, a strikingly attractive redhead with a clear, booming voice, approached one male guest after another and drew them into her performance. With equal amounts of good humor, sexy interplay, and musical talent the beguiling redhead tore away the inhibitions of more and more of Margaret's guests. As the evening progressed, the lead singer increasingly added to the number of attendees involved in the evening's musical entertainment. At one point, a few of the female guests complained to Margaret that the guys were receiving all of the attention from the entertainers. Their complaints did not fall on deaf ears. Following the band's next break, the handsome bass guitarist stepped down from the makeshift stage. He sang to and danced with every woman within thirty feet of the stage.

The party was a roaring success as evidenced by the noise level and the lack of any early departures. Throughout the evening a chorus of voices could be heard singing along with some of the early rock n' roll classics. On more than one occasion Margaret was astonished as she observed people, who only hours before had been strangers, draped familiarly around each other. She took this to be a good sign. Margaret knew that hosting an event like this was an effective way to solidify existing clients and even cultivate potential ones. She handed out a number of business cards during the evening and saw guests exchange their own cards as the attendees mingled. This is not to say that the evening did not have a few troubling moments. She grew a little put out with her husband, who spent the majority of the evening pigeon-holed in a living room corner with his project team from work. On the plus side, she finally had the opportunity to connect a face to the names of his closely knit project team. There was Jay Stewart, a balding, studious type, probably in his mid-twenties, and Becky Archer, a rea-sonably attractive blonde who appeared to be straight out of graduate school. Becky had an annoying habit of laughing too loudly at any-thing remotely comical that Brad or Jay said. Margaret pictured her husband acting as mentor to both of these individuals in addition to his position as team leader on recent projects.

At a few minutes past one o'clock the party began to wind down. Although the band concluded playing around eleven thirty, Margaret was pleased to see two members of the Pulsating Beats still on the premises. She could not help but notice that Susan, the talented lead singer, was standing arm and arm with Dr. Joshua Daley. Margaret was reminded of the old adage about how opposites attract.

Eventually, Margaret found herself sitting by the fireplace in the living room, a glass of brandy and eggnog in hand. Next to her sat Claire Gagnon from the Chamber of Commerce office. It was well after one o'clock and Margaret could hear sporadic laughter from up-stairs as Brad gave Jay and Becky a tour of the house. Margaret was proud of their house. She picked up on the pride in Brad's voice as he described the thought process that went into planning the layout of the rooms and the current furnishings in them. Although pleased to hear the enthusiasm in his voice, a part of her resented that he was receiv-ing all the kudos, considering it was her income that made the pur-chase of the house possible.

"You and Brad seem to have your own separate circle of friends," injected Claire. Claire was Margaret's closest friend and the person she turned to whenever she needed a sounding board on business or personal matters.

"Brad spends a lot of time on the road with these people. As you can see they have become a pretty close-knit trio over the last six months. I think it's good they get along so well. Brad would probably be miserable by now if he were spending all of this time with a couple of SOBs."

"If I may ask, does he resent what you've managed to put together in the last couple of years?" asked Claire. The question caught Margaret a little off guard. Even though she and Claire were close, Margaret was an extremely private person in the area of personal finances.

"Brad is very supportive. He has never been threatened by my ambition. He appears to love his work and is quite successful in his own right. We've had discussions about my need for independence and my entrepreneurial drive. He doesn't share my need to be self-employed and in charge. He says he is very content working for someone else. You know, Claire, thinking back to the early years building my practice—I'm not sure I would have had the same courage to go out on my own in the first place if it weren't for his regular paycheck coming in every week."

"I'm glad to hear it," added Claire. "It sounds like you two really suit each other. Do you happen to know of any others floating around like him?"

"I can introduce you to Jay," mused Margaret playfully.

"A little too young and maybe a bit too intellectual for my taste."

The two women looked up to see Brad escorting Jay and Becky over to say goodnight.

"Oh, I'm sorry you're leaving so soon, we've barely had time to speak all evening," said Margaret to her husband's young assistants. She was speaking in complete sincerity. "I hope I can get you back over to the house real soon so I can spend some time with you," she added. The two guests smiled but did not jump on the invitation.

"You really have a beautiful house, Mrs. Olson," said Becky, almost in a whisper. Margaret suspected that the young woman was a little intimidated by her.

"Mrs. Olson!" exclaimed Margaret. "No dear, Brad's mother is Mrs. Olson! It makes me sound so old. Please, just call me Margaret." She glanced over at Jay who seemed hard-pressed to add anything to the conversation.

"So Jay, I notice you're not wearing a wedding ring. Does that mean I can play matchmaker or are you involved at the moment?" said Margaret, still showing remarkable energy at this late hour. The question caught the young man by surprise and he groped for a witty response. None was forthcoming.

"No, I'm quite single. With all the time we spend on projects out of town, it seems most of the women I meet live hundreds of miles away or more."

"I'm surprised you haven't snapped him up, Becky," said Margaret, glancing at the petite blonde. The comment brought a chuckle from Claire.

"Listen, dear," interrupted Brad. "I'm going to walk these two to their cars. I'll be back in a few seconds."

As Brad disappeared out the front door with his youthful associates, Margaret helped Claire on with her coat.

"I suppose I should thank you for not trying to line me up with J.J. I saw that devilish look in your eye." Claire spoke with her usual elegant, lightheartedness.

"Oh come on, Claire, that would have been a bit much. I'm sure you're here alone tonight of your own volition. I can't even imagine you having a problem in that area," added Margaret.

It was true. Claire Gagnon, standing just under six feet on a slender frame, was the kind of woman who could practically pick the man of her choice. Her long, black hair framed a pair of deep, blue eyes that could draw a man from across a crowded room with a glance. Claire could give the sort of look that prompts a man to risk having his ego shattered just on the chance that she might share a conversation with him.

"Thanks again for all the help tonight. Will I see you again before the holidays?" asked Margaret.

"Let's play it by ear. I'll give you a call at the office next week. In the meantime, keep your eyes open for an eligible bachelor that you can fix me up with. Oh, and stop hiring all of those studious-looking pinheads for the office, and for once bring in someone worth calling me over to check out. There's got to be at least one sexy accountant out there for your very best friend," joked Claire.

Margaret laughed and gave her friend a quick hug before sending her down the long driveway to the road. She heard Brad laughing a short distance away, but decided to duck back into the house before catching a cold for Christmas. Jenny, who helped most of the evening serving food and drinks, was upstairs in her bedroom, probably asleep. The few remaining guests were now filtering out the door, each generous with their compliments for the hostess. After graciously accepting the last of many kudos, Margaret began the long process of cleaning off table tops, and straightening furniture. The dishwasher was loaded and in operation when Brad finally returned to the house.

"Jesus, what did you people do out there, read *War and Peace* together?" barked Margaret sarcastically. She was put out with Brad and she was not going to waste any time before letting him know it.

"Hey, I won't be seeing Jay until after New Year's Day. I was going over some things with him and Becky."

"And what's the story with her? The way you talked about those two I pictured something a little more polished. I really have a problem visualizing them functioning in your work environment," snapped Margaret.

"It's clear to me that you just want to fight. What is your problem?" asked Brad. He spoke deliberately.

"Well, now that you ask, my problem is that you weren't much goddamn help tonight! I ran my ass off around here and for the most part, you were hiding out with your little friends. I guess that's my problem." With the last of her guests gone from the house Margaret was free to bark at her husband at full volume.

"Just a reminder—the party was your idea, not mine. It was for your benefit, not mine. And in case you didn't notice, the guests were ninety-five percent your friends and precious business clients, not mine. And, if you don't mind, I'm going to bed. Goodnight!" Brad turned and ascended the stairs. Margaret became unsettled. Brad seemed uncharacteristically cold and short with her.

Margaret returned to picking up the living room. It was going to take five or six cycles of the dishwasher to make any headway on the plates and glasses. Many would have to be returned to the rental store Monday morning. Margaret decided to put off any major offensive on the clutter until the morning. Returning to the living room, she collapsed onto the sofa in front of the television set. She was not ready to join Brad in the bedroom so, picking up the TV remote, she began flipping through the fifty-eight channels. She raced from program to program, not stopping for more than a few seconds on any single station. Then, realizing that she was doing exactly what she so often criticized her husband and daughter for, Margaret stopped on VH1. She thought how a few hours earlier the living room was vibrating with the sound of music, voices and laughter. Now it was quiet and empty.

Inexplicably, Margaret was feeling desperately alone. It was not just because Brad was upstairs sulking, or that Jenny was sound asleep in her room. It was something more. She felt detached from everyone in her life. Brad was on the road so much lately, and even when he was home it seemed she was putting in marathon hours at the office herself. Jenny was seventeen and spending more and more time out of the house with her friends. In nine months Jenny would be leaving to attend college. Margaret found herself coming down with a case of the holiday blues. She raised the volume on the TV set at the sight of Rod Stewart:

> *You're in my heart, you're in my soul*
> *You'll be my breath should I grow old*
> *You are my lover, you're my best friend*
> *You're in my soul*

A tired smile broke out on Margaret's face as Rod Stewart's raspy tones brought back some tender memories. She thought of times that could never return. It was a time when her joy for living had no relationship to her bank account or her personal financial statement. These were times that would never return. Her thoughts were becoming too unpleasant to bear. Margaret flipped off the downstairs lights and started up the stairs. Once again she thought back to that Christmas seventeen years before and her brief conversation with Brian Kelly. She hoped he was having a happy Christmas season this year, wherever he was.

There were no apologies the next morning. Everything was just forgotten. Brad spent a little more time around the house over the holidays while Margaret prepared for another tax season. Brad was scheduled to leave for Columbia, Maryland on a business trip the second week of January.

4

ON A SUNDAY EVENING IN EARLY JANUARY, Brad Olson quietly entered his wife's home office and sat in the upholstered chair next to her mahogany desk. Her back was to him as she prepared a memo on the computer. After a few seconds of silence she turned to her husband. Margaret noticed a pained look on his face.

"Are you okay?" she asked.

"I'm afraid I'm here to do something that is so difficult. I don't even know how to start."

"Jesus, Brad, you're scaring me. What's wrong?" asked Margaret, her voice beginning to reflect the sudden tension in the room.

"I'm moving out of the house and finding an apartment down in Massachusetts—something closer to work. I need some time away from here to sort things out." He spoke in a monotone manner, giving the impression that his words had been rehearsed. Margaret only stared at him for the next few seconds. She was momentarily speechless. His words sent a shockwave through her nervous system.

"It has nothing to do with anything you did or didn't do. It's just the only way I have to deal with the fact that I am so incredibly unhappy." The monotone quality in his voice was gone now. Brad Olson sounded genuinely sorry.

"Are you sleeping with someone?" asked Margaret accusingly. Brad gave no response other than dropping his eyes to the floor and weakly nodding in the affirmative.

"You fucking bastard!" she screamed. Jumping from behind her desk Margaret moved toward him, slapping him on the side of his face and head. He made no attempt to defend himself aside from leaning away from the force of her blows.

"What are you trying to do to me?" she bellowed.

"I told you, Margaret, it has nothing to do with you. It has everything to do with me."

"Nothing to do with me. It's got everything to do with me. Listen to me—if you walk out on me like this, I promise, I vow I will take everything you have, everything. You know I can—and you know I will." She was speaking slowly and purposefully.

"I don't want anything, Margaret. It's more yours than mine anyway. You paid for most of it—you keep it. Just my car and my clothes, that's all I need." Brad was speaking calmly and softly.

"If you walk out on me tonight, I will never—never take you back," she threatened.

He extended his hand toward her but she brushed it aside and returned to behind her desk. By this time Margaret had begun to cry. It was a low, controlled sobbing that she drew into herself. Brad was already making his way to the door.

"How can you do this to me? What's wrong with you?" she asked, her voice was taking on a pathetic quality.

"We'll be able to discuss this more rationally in a few days. I'll call you from Maryland. Please, Margaret, this doesn't mean that I don't really care for you and Jenny. I just have to do this for myself." As Brad began to open the door to leave, Margaret whispered a final appeal.

"Brad, please don't do this—please don't leave me alone."

"I'm so sorry," he answered in a low mumble, choking back his emotions. As he closed the door behind him his eyes met Jenny's. She was standing across the hallway in front of her bedroom, her eyes wide and awash in tears. She did not speak. Brad could only drop his head and descend the stairs to the front door. Moments later there came the sound of his car driving off into the evening.

5

THE OFFICES OF MARGARET KEOGH-OLSON, Certified Public Accountant, were located in downtown Manchester, New Hampshire, in a
stately group of brick office buildings built at the end of the nine-
teenth century. Although extensively restored in the past twelve months,
the interior of the building retained much of the charm and quaintness
of the preceding century. The wooden window casements and floors,
low ceilings, elaborate stairway banisters, and numerous fireplaces
throughout the two-and-a-half story building were preserved by Margaret during the restoration, in spite of opposition from the contractor.
She intentionally kept the individual offices small during the renovation process, simply because it felt right to her. If anyone persisted in
questioning her decision during renovation, she politely reminded them
who would be paying the mortgage every month and closed the discussion.

Margaret arrived at work early, even by her standards, on this cold,
January morning. She had not slept well in the half-empty bed the
night before. On the drive in from Bedford she struggled with a difficult question. Should Brad's decision to move out the night before be
made common knowledge? Pulling into her assigned parking space,
she made up her mind not to discuss it with anyone in the office, at
least not yet.

Although Margaret had left the maddening world of the "Big Six"
accounting firms just seven years earlier, she managed to expand her
practice from that of a sole practitioner to an office with five college-
educated accountants, two certified, in her employ, and a clerical staff
of two full-time and one part-time individuals. She built her practice
through a strategy of relentless networking with an ever-expanding
number of local professionals. She went to great lengths to develop

relationships within the legal community which, in turn, provided her with a stream of constant referrals. Finally, on a more basic and primitive level, Margaret was quite aware of her own physical attributes. She was a physically attractive and tremendously fit woman. Men enjoyed her company, professionally and socially, and she used this to facilitate business growth.

Margaret was not surprised to find the office silent and empty as she unlocked the front door and simultaneously turned off the building alarm. She climbed the stairs and proceeded down the hallway to her office in the corner of the building. For her, this would be another indiscernible day in a procession of twelve-to-fourteen-hour workdays. It was the beginning of tax season and it was unavoidable. For Margaret, mid-January to April 15 had come to mean a schedule of sixty-five to seventy billable hours per week, not to mention the additional, countless, non-billable ones. It meant meeting constant deadlines, personal difficulty sleeping, meetings with short-tempered employees, argumentative clients, and lots of coffee. She could bank on plenty of fast food and stress levels high enough to turn her personal physician gray. Tax season often meant spending more time conversing with IRS agents than with family members. Margaret knew full well that, until mid-April, such things as renting videos, casual reading, television, and most any other form of socializing were out of the question. However, she left herself one daily recreational activity—her forty-five minute workout and run at the health club every noon. She justified it as necessary for ongoing physical and mental health.

When Margaret Keogh-Olson was not managing the financial and tax affairs of the most demanding and profitable clients in the office, she was scheduling and reviewing the work of her professional staff. It was her name on the shingle and Margaret made a point of reviewing as much of the work produced by her staff as was humanly possible. This was not only the case for her young, inexperienced college grads, but also for the two CPAs working out of the office. Margaret worked harder and longer than anyone else in the organization.

That first day was painful, but soon Margaret was swept up into the distractions of work. By March it became clear to her that a half day off a week, Sunday morning, was not enough. She became aware of her own mental and physical deterioration. In late March the weather was beginning to warm up. Back in January, she had told herself that Brad would recover his senses, weather his mid-life crisis, and crawl back to her by spring. However, he had not returned home by the first day of spring and, on this day, Margaret received word that her husband had moved in with Becky Archer. Word of this development made her feel foolish.

Margaret sat behind her desk on a Friday night. The building was quiet and empty, and had been for hours. Tomorrow was her birthday. She would be thirty-four years old. Thirty-four going on eighty-four, she thought. Jesus, where was her life going? She got up from her desk and walked across the room to a small mirror in the corner. Her eyes ached and she was tired. Throwing back her head she stared at herself. There were deep circles under her eyes and her face seemed drawn. Margaret thought she looked older than she was. She thought of how she could rest herself in just two and a half weeks. Was she burning out or just overtired? Margaret glanced down at the clock on her desk. Ten thirty-five. She considered her situation. She was alone in the office at ten thirty-five on a Friday night. She left everything strewn across her desk as it was, and left for home.

Margaret was mulling over a few touchy matters at the office as she robotically drove back to Bedford this night. Turning the car up the driveway, she hoped Jenny would still be up. Flickering light images were visible through the front window, indicating to Margaret that her daughter was probably watching television. Entering the front door, she saw Jenny rolled in a tight ball on the couch.

"Hi, Jen, how are things on the home front?" she asked as usual.

"Okay, Mom, just waiting up for you. I think I was dozing off," answered Jenny in a sweet way, making her mother's arrival home all the more pleasant. Margaret made her way straight to the kitchen.

"How about joining your poor, half-dead mother for a hot chocolate before I pass out from exhaustion?"

"Sure, sounds great. Let me see if I can find some of those little marshmallows we bought a while back." Jenny began twirling the lazy Susan in the corner of the kitchen as her search began. Jenny Keogh was taller and more angular than her mother with a pretty, kittenish face. There was a strong, facial resemblance between the two, although Margaret's features were unquestionably more sharp and defined.

"Oh, Mom, there's a message for you over by the phone. Some guy called a couple of hours ago. He said he knew something about a friend of yours, and if you were interested to call him back. His number's there."

"Knows something about a friend of mine?" repeated Margaret. She glanced across the room at her daughter as a confused expression spread over her face. Reaching over Jenny's shoulder, Margaret snatched the bag of mini-marshmallows from an upper shelf. She walked to the kitchen phone and focused on the lone message thumbtacked above the telephone. It read—Rory O'Shea. She stared at the pink WHILE YOU WERE OUT sheet for a full five seconds before looking back to Jenny.

"Do you know who he is?" questioned her daughter.

"Yes—yes I do," she responded. "I'll call him back in the morning."

Joining her daughter at the kitchen table, Margaret asked about school, graduation plans and anything else that came to mind. She reminded Jenny that tax season would soon be over and they would be able to return to their normal, mother-daughter relationship. However, even as she spoke to her daughter, Margaret entertained thoughts of the call from Rory O'Shea. They finished their warm drinks and escorted each other upstairs. Jenny had not mentioned her birthday. Margaret wondered if she had forgotten. She kissed her daughter goodnight and retired to her bedroom. Once alone, she was able to carefully consider the possibilities this call from her former classmate opened up. Rory left a message that he knew something about a friend of hers. She started worrying, fearing the news from Rory O'Shea might not be good, but it was too late to call.

As Margaret reached to turn off her light she thought of the diary. Pulling open the drawer in her night stand, she took out the battered manuscript for the first time in nearly three months.

March 30, 1973

Dear Diary...Brian told me to listen to WFEA tonight during Johnny Tripp's show. Just after the eight o'clock news Johnny Tripp says he's dedicating a song to Bedford's original heartbreaker...Maggie May Keogh...on her sixteenth birthday...and then he plays Maggie May. Brian probably had to bring him a hundred cheeseburgers to get him to say that. I called Brian and thanked him.

She drifted off to sleep thinking about Brian, wondering what information Rory would pass on to her. Could Brian Kelly actually be living a short distance away? Did she have the courage to call, or drop in on him, if he was?

* * *

Margaret arrived at the office at nine-thirty the following morning. Three hours earlier, she had been delighted to find a wrapped birthday present from Jenny on the kitchen table. Margaret, in turn, hung around and had breakfast with her daughter before leaving the house. The rest of the staff was already at work when she arrived. Margaret took a few minutes to touch base with each one and get a status report on where they stood with their workload. Once that was completed, she slipped back to her office, closed the door, and called Rory O'Shea.

"Hello," said a male voice.

"Hi, Rory? This is Margaret Keogh returning your call."

"Maggie, you just caught me going out the door," said Rory. She cringed at being called Maggie but did not correct her high school acquaintance.

"Well listen, I have a moment. You told me to let you know if I ever heard anything about Brian's whereabouts and that's exactly what I'm doing. This is wild. I'm playing cards the other night with the same crowd as always and Louie Bruneau is telling us how he and his wife had spent a weekend at Wells Beach the week before. He's going on about how cheap it was with the off-season rates and all, and then he says he met up with an old friend of mine at the inn where he stayed. It turns out that Brian runs the place or works there or some-thing. Louie was never very close to Brian, but he remembered him and told him he played cards with me every week. Anyway, Brian told him to tell me to give him a ring or drop by if I'm ever in the area. Isn't that wild? That happening after you called me about him only a few months ago?"

"Did you happen to get Brian's address or phone number?" asked Margaret, still stunned by this revelation.

"Well, almost—I do know that he works at the Atlantic Coast Lodge, on Route 1, in Wells, Maine. It sounds like a pretty good-sized place to hear Louie talk. I don't have the phone number, but I imagine you could get it from directory assistance. Anyway Maggie, I promised I'd let you know if I ever heard anything—and now I've delivered on my promise."

Margaret thanked Rory for remembering her call from the previous summer and wrapped up their conversation quickly. She immediately dialed directory assistance in Maine. Thirty seconds later, Margaret Keogh-Olson had Brian Kelly's work number scribbled on a note pad in front of her. She transferred the number onto the back of one of her business cards and tucked it into her briefcase. She called Claire at home and arranged a luncheon date on Monday at the Portsmouth Fish House, their favorite seafood restaurant in Manchester. There were a couple of matters she wanted to run by her best friend. One was the rationality of a plan to drive over to Maine and visit her old friend from Southside High School.

6

THE FOLLOWING MONDAY, Margaret arrived at the Portsmouth Fish House, a quiet, intimate restaurant in the city's business district, and claimed a booth by the window. Moments later she watched as Claire pulled up in her Volvo, found a parking space near the front door, and strolled up to the restaurant. Entering the front door, Claire scanned the dining area for her friend, as every set of male eyes shifted in her direction. Margaret made a hand gesture, catching her friend's attention, and soon Claire joined her in the booth. They exchanged pleasantries and swapped rumors about common acquaintances within the local business community. Eventually Margaret steered the conversation toward what she needed to discuss with her confidante.

"You've got to tell me if you think I'm crazy about something I'm seriously considering to do in a couple of weeks," said Margaret. Claire's eyes widened.

"When tax season ends I'm thinking of packing a suitcase and heading over to Maine—alone. I've managed to locate my old friend, Brian Kelly, and I'm thinking of dropping in on him, totally unannounced." Margaret took a bite of lunch and waited for her friend's reaction.

"Wait a minute, I'm lost," answered Claire, a bewildered look breaking over her face. "Who is Brian Kelly?"

"Remember last summer, I told you about coming across this old diary of mine from high school and reading about my last year at Southside High, and everything I went through carrying Jenny and all. Brian was the guy that had really liked me!"

"Now I remember, you found out you had slighted him over something. Jesus, Margaret, you're not still thinking about that and blaming yourself, are you?" asked Claire in astonishment.

"Claire, his friend called me last week and told me where he works at a hotel or lodge or something in Wells, Maine—I have his number—and I'm very seriously thinking of going up to see him."

"Margaret, you haven't seen this guy since high school, it's been fifteen years!" Claire said mockingly.

"More like seventeen—but who's counting?"

It was evident to Claire that her friend had done the math. Claire searched Margaret's face for a sign of what was driving her. Methodically she took a sip from her water glass before continuing. She softened her tone.

"Aren't you afraid he might just tell you to go to hell or something? What if he's married and you run into his wife?"

"I'm not going up there to screw him, Claire! There's just this thing I have to resolve with him. I feel a little guilty—no, very guilty—about something that happened back then and I want to apologize. Besides, he's not the vindictive type."

Claire saw that her friend's nerves were on edge; Margaret was overreacting to a very simple inquiry.

"You don't know him anymore, Margaret. It's been a long time since you've seen him. I'm just saying that it's hard to know what to expect," added Claire.

"He's not the kind of guy who would just change. I'm fairly sure of that. Anyway, I just wanted your take on all of this and now I have it. I'll give it a little bit more thought but I'm pretty sure I'll be going up to Maine." Margaret resumed picking at her meal and the table grew quiet for a short while. Their friendship was solid enough to allow for silence at moments like this without creating discomfort. Gradually the conversation resumed before Margaret's demeanor again grew serious, this time about another matter.

"I'm considering letting Vern Butler go at the end of tax season," Margaret confided without lifting her gaze. Claire gasped as she focused her attention from across the table.

"Why?"

"I haven't said anything, at his request, up until now but the whole situation is beginning to do me in. His wife, Sarah, has been undergoing radiation treatment for the past few weeks now and he's been out of the office more than he's been in. Needless to say, this couldn't have come at a worse time, tax season and all. I've been forced to pick up the slack. I'm already worn out and Vern's already talking about some further treatment for her if the radiation doesn't work. I've got to take some action on this because this whole fucking thing is wearing me out." Margaret's voice cracked under the stress of just talking about the circumstances. She sipped at her water and resumed.

"You know, Claire, it's not like my life is a fucking bed of roses right now. I just have to get out from under some of this shit." Claire was about to remind her friend of Vern's contribution to her success but decided against it.

"I'm worn out from the office and from this crap from Brad. I have to start easing up on myself or I'll be going over the edge." Margaret was speaking with such uninhibited frankness that Claire knew this decision was causing her real anguish.

"It sounds like you've probably given this a lot of thought. I'm sure you wouldn't do it unless you knew you absolutely had to."

Claire reached across the table and squeezed her friend's hand. "Take it easy on yourself and do whatever it will take to get yourself back on track," she suggested, with an understanding tone in her voice. For the remainder of the meal less stressful matters were discussed until the two parted at the front door in the midst of an early spring downpour.

It was late in the afternoon on April 12th when Margaret summoned Vern Butler to her office and informed him that his services were being terminated. She delivered her unexpected decision in a firm, emotionless voice, barely lifting her eyes from her desk. She explained to her employee of six years that his wife's health problems had taken their toll on her and the business, as well as his family. She explained that she had concluded that this action had to be taken. Margaret promised Vern that she would continue to carry the Butlers on the firm's health plan until Sarah's immediate health problems were resolved. In addition, she extended him three months' severance pay in recognition of his six years of service. Margaret asked him to remain on until the end of the month in order to bring his clients' records up to date and to allow for a smooth transition.

The meeting took less than twenty minutes. To Margaret's relief, Vern took the news calmly, at least on the surface. At no time did the proud, middle-aged professional attempt to plead for his position or even offer excuses. He accepted the fact that his services were no longer needed. Margaret informed him that nothing would be said to the other employees until he had cleared his office and totally removed himself from the practice. He thanked her for her generous severance package and dutifully withdrew from the office.

Standing at her office window, Margaret Keogh-Olson watched as Vern Butler walked to his car. She pulled away and returned to her desk at the sight of the proud man's departure. She reassured herself that she had handled the matter quite professionally. They both had, she thought. Margaret reminded herself that she would be leaving for Maine in less than seventy-two hours. The thought of a getaway lifted her spirits.

April 15th fell on Monday and Margaret made no attempt to burn the midnight oil. Instead, she left for home at four o'clock in the afternoon after being assured that extensions had been filed for each and every client in need of one. She scheduled the staff member with the least seniority to stay at the office and man the phones until nine o'clock that evening in the event of an emergency call from an existing or potential client. Margaret and Jenny went out to dinner this night. They kept the conversation upbeat and light. No talk of work, college, Brad, Jenny's grades, nothing that could cause even the least amount of friction. It was just a long overdue mother-daughter evening out. Jenny's response to her mother's planned trip to Maine was enthusiastic. Margaret thought it was wise to share her plans with as few people as possible, but Jenny did not fall under her informational blackout. However, Margaret thought it prudent to make no mention of Brian. Jenny's grandparents had been invited to stay at the house with Jenny during Margaret's absence.

7

FOLLOWING A SOLID NIGHT'S SLEEP, Margaret made her way to the kitchen early Tuesday morning and prepared blueberry pancakes and last minute instructions for her daughter. It was April 16 and tax season was over. In a few hours she would be heading due east toward the Atlantic Ocean on Route 101. Suddenly the reality hit her that it was no longer a plan or a daydream. Margaret realized that if she was to be reunited with Brian it was time for action. She mulled over Claire's cautionary advice from lunch the previous week. Dropping in unannounced could prove to be a disaster. What if she had to confront a Mrs. Kelly before even speaking to Brian? What if he simply dismissed her? A feeling of anxiety created one question after another in Margaret's thoughts. As she packed the last article into her suitcase, she consoled herself with the thought that there was nothing stopping her from just driving by the Atlantic Coast Lodge when the time came.

With the car finally packed and the house secured, a wave of exhilaration swept over her. Margaret pulled her BMW out of the driveway and headed east. She had no timetable and no real itinerary. For the next few days Margaret would not allow herself to be burdened with responsibilities or worries. Momentarily, she sat motionless behind the wheel of her car, a smile set on her face. It struck her that she was absolutely, positively, unequivocally free! She sped eastward on Route 101 until it intersected with the interstate; then it was northward through Portsmouth until, at long last, the state of Maine. Once in the Pine Tree State, she left the highway after a short distance. Minutes later, she was browsing through the clothing outlets and specialty stores in Kittery. In one boutique, she spotted a casual, artsy cap that she instinctively knew Jenny would love. On impulse she purchased it, and an identical one for herself. The cap remained in the shopping bag only until she reached her car. Moments later, Margaret Olson was cruising up Route 1 toward Wells, her artsy, bohemian cap tilted to one side of her head. Soon she developed an appetite, and, finding all of the seafood stands still closed for the season, she pulled into a hot dog stand in York. Margaret figured a light lunch would keep the hunger pains away until that evening, when she planned to feast on Maine lobster and steamers. At the weather-beaten hot dog stand, Margaret learned that Wells was only seven or eight miles up the road.

As soon as she passed the Wells town line, Margaret began scanning both sides of the road for the Atlantic Coast Lodge. Route 1 seemed vaguely familiar, even after so many years. This was her first visit back to the area since her summer with Brian. Driving northward, she caught a glimpse of the ocean on her right in the distance. Margaret saw clearly from the businesses lining Route 1 that the southern coast of Maine was tourist country. Fortunately for her, the road was practically deserted. This was understandable—it was midday, midweek, in the off season. Up ahead, she caught sight of a sign that read "Mile Road." A red traffic light brought her to a stop, allowing her to get her bearings. Pulling ahead from the intersection, her eyes scanned right and spotted the sign:

ATLANTIC COAST LODGE

ENTER HERE

Margaret felt a knot crop up in her stomach as she turned her BMW into the driveway through an opening in a stockade fence. The car rolled forward into the complex and she focused on a large house set in the middle of the grounds. A rustic sign read BED AND BREAKFAST. The white building sat in the midst of a thick, plush lawn, not yet green, and was further encircled by small and medium-sized cottages. There appeared to be a motel set back behind the main lodge. Methodically, she pulled the car into one of the parking spaces designated for registering guests and shut off the engine. She was apprehensive over the pending reunion. She reassured herself that she could still back up and drive away. Instead, following a few deep breaths, Margaret stepped out of the car and started toward the entrance to the lodge. While reaching for the doorknob, Margaret realized she had not checked her appearance in the mirror. What he sees is what he gets, she thought, and stepped through the door.

The registration area was dominated by a neat, knotty-pine counter with light provided by a green half-cylinder shade attached to a brass base—something Margaret thought of as a "library lamp." At the moment, no one was there to greet her, and no sign of Brian. Margaret glanced to her left and saw a hospitality area consisting of a spacious, carpeted room, with eight or nine big comfortable chairs forming a half circle. In the corner, a television set was tuned to a soap opera. Seconds passed, then came the sound of footsteps descending the stairs from the second floor. Margaret froze as a figure appeared from the bottom of the stairwell. But, it wasn't Brian, it was a woman who appeared to be in her mid-sixties.

"Oh, I'm sorry. I didn't hear you come in. How long have you been standing there?" asked the woman in a kindly voice.

"Only a few moments," replied Margaret in a relaxed tone, letting the woman know she was not upset.

"You know, you could have rung the little bell on the desk. Course if you're like me, you feel a little pushy, pounding on them things— like you're so important and can't be kept waiting." The gray-haired woman gave out a spontaneous laugh and glanced outside at Margaret's car.

"Will you be staying with us tonight?"

"Yes, I was wondering what you had available. I have no reservation or anything." The woman erupted in laughter.

"My dear, at this time of year you don't need a reservation, that's for sure. We can offer you a cottage or a motel unit on the hill overlooking the harbor, or you can stay right here in the lodge, and join us down here in the morning for breakfast."

"That sounds very nice. I'll take a room right here in the lodge," responded Margaret, already getting a comfortable feeling from her amiable hostess. Still, there was no sign of Brian.

"I can offer you the forties, fifties or sixties room. The seventies room is taken."

"Pardon me. Are those the prices?" asked Margaret, totally confused.

"No dear, I'm sorry, those are the decades in which the rooms are decorated. Our owner thought it was a novel idea to furnish the rooms based on a decade. Some of our guests get a big kick out of it. The furniture, the artwork, the reading material, the radios, the whole shooting match. Personally, I think it's a little silly but, then again, I'm not paid to think," sang out the likable woman.

"Well, it's different. That's for sure," said Margaret.

"Okay, if the seventies room is taken, then how about the sixties room?" asked Margaret. The matronly woman gave her a sideways look and wrinkled her nose, indicating that her choice was a poor one. Margaret understood.

"On second thought, how about the fifties room?" Margaret said with amusement.

"You won't get an argument from me on that choice. In fact, it's my personal favorite. There's a wonderful picture of Eisenhower in there."

"Well, I like Ike," retorted Margaret as she began to get caught up in the hospitable banter with the innkeeper. She was halfway through filling in the registration form when she decided to slip in the question foremost in her mind.

"Does Brian Kelly still work here?" she inquired, attempting to sound as casual as possible

"He sure does, but he won't be back until sometime this evening. He's up in Augusta attending some meetings on tourism. I expect him around seven. He's got to be back for eleven when I leave. Do you know Brian?"

"We were in school together back in New Hampshire," answered Margaret.

"Well, you got me there. I didn't even know Brian ever lived in New Hampshire," replied the older woman. "Did he know you were coming?"

"Oh no, he didn't. It's really no big deal," answered Margaret defensively.

"By the way, I don't think I introduced myself. I'm Millie."

"And I'm Margaret Olson, but I guess you knew that from my registration card." Margaret extended her hand out of habit, causing Millie to respond. The gesture caught the older woman off guard.

"Millie, may I run upstairs and take a peek at my room?" she asked with almost girlish enthusiasm.

"Of course you can, dear—top of the stairs—to the end of the hall. It has 'fifties' marked right on the door."

Taking the key from Millie, Margaret proceeded up the stairs and to the end of the hall. She opened the door to find a large, sunny room with two windows on the far wall. The windows provided a delightful view of Wells Harbor and the Atlantic Ocean. Margaret smiled as she scanned the room, taking note of its decorations. The room's queen-sized bed appeared to be made of oak, complete with a built-in bookshelf. She walked over and collapsed on the bed. Gazing up at the row of hardcover books, she read off *Peyton Place, The Human Comedy, Catcher in the Rye, On the Road, Atlas Shrugged, The Old Man and the Sea*, and the *Holy Bible*. She wondered what role Brian had in the selection process. Across the room on the bureau was a plastic, cylinder-shaped lamp depicting Niagara Falls. In one corner of the room, a small picture of Marilyn Monroe. In the other, a color portrait of Dwight Eisenhower. The urge to unload the car and unpack her things struck Margaret.

Margaret descended the stairs and stepped outside to unload her luggage. She caught Millie's eye on her last trip past the desk.

"Oh Millie, by any chance do Brian and his family live close by?" She knew the question was awkward and a little too obvious the moment she said it, but it was the best she could come up with. Millie looked up from her paperwork, a slightly puzzled expression covered her face.

"What family is that, dear?"

"You know, his wife and children. He's got to be married by now," responded Margaret sheepishly.

"Brian's your typical confirmed bachelor, unless he's got some secrets back in New Hampshire we don't know about," mused the woman with a sarcastic chuckle.

Margaret smiled and returned to her room with the last of her luggage. She looked out over the harbor, as Brian must have on countless occasions over the years. It was almost too good to be true, she thought. If she were able to spend some time with her old friend, she knew it would definitely be without placating the fears of a jealous wife.

After unpacking and putting away her toiletries, Margaret decided to explore the area since Brian was not expected back until sometime in the evening. She drove due east on Mile Road toward the Atlantic. She was intrigued by the sight of a freestanding seafood restaurant on the way to the ocean, sitting alone and surrounded by acres of protected marshland and estuary. She made a mental note to walk there for dinner some evening. Continuing eastward, she reached the ocean no more than a minute later. It was the off season so she was able to pull the car into a parking spot overlooking the crashing surf. Margaret emerged from the car and stood against a chain-link fence as the cool wind blew her hair almost horizontally. At this moment, everything felt right to her. Again, Margaret asked herself how Brian would react to her after all this time? In any event, the worst-case scenario was that she would at least be able to clear her conscience over the misunderstanding from so many Christmases ago. Margaret reminded herself that she was visiting Brian Kelly, not some ogre. She reassured herself that everything would be okay.

After a few minutes spent leaning against the fence, Margaret hopped back in the BMW and set out to fully explore the area, taking time to map out the local terrain. Margaret quickly learned that there were two sides to Wells, Maine. There was the Route 1 community that ran parallel to the Atlantic Ocean, a mile west of the sea. The topography consisted of an elevated ridge that provided a view of the ocean and harbor from between an unbroken line of motels, restaurants, gas stations, and antique shops. At the edge of the Atlantic was the Wells Beach community. Its geography was made up of a narrow strip of land, the soil of which provided the foundation for the finest vacation properties in the town. If the Wells community on Route 1 was over-commercialized, then it could be said that the Wells Beach community was under-commercialized. A couple of restaurants, a handful of gift shops, a small arcade and two major motels was the extent of commercialism by the edge of the sea. What this strip of land two miles in length and barely a hundred yards in width did have was an expanse of sandy shore. Then, lastly, there was something else that made the town unique. Between Route 1 on the ridge and Wells Beach at the shore was a half-mile-wide buffer of marshland and saltwater estuary. This barren, treeless acreage was crisscrossed by watery passageways that emptied to its muddy floor at low tide, and filled to depths of up to ten feet at high tide. Margaret took it all in as she leisurely cruised along the streets and through the neighborhoods. She thought how Brian had found a town to settle in with a wonderful quality of life.

Later in the afternoon, Margaret drove north to Kennebunkport and spent a leisurely two hours visiting stores and antique shops. She found time to do some exploration along the coastline, near Walker Point and the George Bush estate. By five o'clock she had the sort of appetite that only crisp, ocean air could deliver. She wandered into an intimate restaurant in Kennebunkport's Dock Square and dined alone, all the while rehearsing what she might say to Brian later in the evening.

It was just after six o'clock when Margaret started back to Wells. Driving back toward Route 1, she mused over how wonderful this day was turning out. She fumbled with the car radio, attempting to find an acceptable local station, and finally came upon the Moody Blues. The local oldies station, she thought to herself.

I wonder where you are...
I wonder if you think about me...
Once upon a time in your wildest dreams...

The lyrics sent an emotional surge through her. Margaret Keogh-Olson was getting back in touch with her feelings.

It was still light when Margaret arrived back in Wells. She drove past the Atlantic Coast Lodge and took Mile Road down to the beach. She decided to walk off dinner with a stroll along the shore. She passed a few couples, all elderly, as she journeyed south as far as the beach would allow. Margaret arrived back at the lodge at sunset. Millie was on the phone when she entered the lobby. Margaret scanned the downstairs rooms for any sign of Brian. There was no sign of him. Millie picked up on Margaret's dilemma and excused herself from her phone conversation.

"Still no sign of him. I'll let him know you're here as soon as he comes in," said Millie.

"No, please, that's all right Millie. I'll see him soon enough. I'm just going to get something to read, and find a comfortable chair in the TV room," answered Margaret.

Climbing the stairs to her room, Margaret picked up the current issue of *The Practical Accountant*. Returning downstairs, she found her chair and curled herself up in a warm ball. Millie came in almost immediately and lit the fireplace. The television was set to what appeared to be the local PBS station, judging from the English melodrama being played out, but Margaret ignored the TV and buried herself in her trade magazine.

8

"You're sleeping in my chair, madam."

Someone was speaking to Margaret as she found herself slowly coming out of a relaxing sleep.

"I'm sorry. What was that?" she replied, still not quite half awake.

"Madam, you are sleeping in my chair. Someone in this flophouse should have advised you that this was my chair." Margaret opened her eyes to see a man seated on the foot stool directly in front of her. She peered through the light glaring in from the lobby until the image of a man gradually came into focus.

"Brian, Brian, it's you." Margaret groped for words but found herself merely staring at Brian and repeating his name. His voice was the same, but he had changed in other ways. His face had matured and filled in a little. His hair was shorter and appeared to be styled. He was clean-shaven. She liked that. However, most of all, he was smiling. It was a genuine smile, not a half smile or an "I want to sell you some insurance" smile—a genuine smile. The sort of smile you cannot fake.

"Did you just get in? What time is it?" Margaret was floundering but did manage to put two sentences together.

"Well, Maggie May, to be completely honest, I've been back for about twenty minutes, and for the past fifteen I've just been sitting here trying to figure out what to do with you. Millie told me the whole story—how you got here with no car, no luggage, no money. Dammit, Maggie, it's really pathetic." Brian was having some fun with Margaret, and at her expense.

"Did you really tell him that, Millie?" she cried out to the next room.

"Millie's gone home so you'll get no help from out there. But I've decided to take pity on you and let you stay in the fifties room tonight, and we'll sort this mess out in the morning." Brian suddenly turned from playful to serious. "It's good to see you after all these years." He spoke with sincerity.

Margaret climbed to her feet and reached out to her friend for a hug. Moments later, the two old friends were in an embrace. Nothing was said for a good thirty seconds until Margaret broke the silence.

"Old friends are the best," she said, looking deep into his eyes.

"I'm delighted you're here, but I'm just a little curious. Why here— and now?" he asked.

"Well, now—because it's the end of tax season and I'm a CPA— and here, because you're here and there was something I had to set straight. It's something from a long time ago, and I thought it was something that should be done in person. How much time do you have?" she asked.

"I've got all night," answered Brian, almost dreamily.

Margaret proceeded to tell Brian of her experience the preceding summer, telling him how she found the diary from her sophomore year in high school. She explained how it stirred up both fond and painful memories of their friendship and how she decided to contact his old friend Rory O'Shea. Margaret concluded her account of these events by explaining to Brian that it was only after a phone call to Rory that she became aware of the death of his mother.

"When I put it all together, I suddenly realized that when you called me that Christmas after we had split up, it was because of your mother. You probably just needed me to talk to. I should've been there for you, but I just didn't know. If I had known about your mother—I would have been there, Brian. It's a terrible excuse, but it's the truth, and I don't know what to say except I'm sorry." Tears were visible in Margaret's eyes as she concluded her account of the events from seventeen years earlier. "Please accept my apology," she said.

"It's all right—it's okay. It was a long time ago, and you were only a kid. There's nothing to forgive." Brian spoke in a quiet, serious tone. He grabbed her hand and applied a gentle squeeze. "How long are you going to be around?" he asked, his mood beginning to lighten.

"Oh, a few days. No more than five," answered Margaret.

"Why don't I take tomorrow off from work. Would you let me show you around southern Maine?"

"Any chance of going back to Parson's Beach?" asked Margaret flirtatiously.

"First thing after breakfast." Brian glanced at his watch and did a double take.

"It's after midnight. I'd better let you sleep in tomorrow morning. I won't knock 'til around eight-thirty. That okay?" he asked.

"That'll be fine," answered Margaret. She reached down for her magazine before making her way back to the second floor. Brian was quick to spot it, and playfully yanked it out of her hand as he escorted her to her room.

"What the hell is this? *The Practical Accountant*? Dammit, Maggie May, could you possibly have come up with a more boring, gag-in-your-mouth piece of reading material? Am I going to get lectured tomorrow for leaving a fifteen-and-a-half-percent tip at breakfast? What do I have to look forward to for conversation? The 'S' corporation versus the 'C' corporation?" Margaret saw the familiar twinkle in Brian's eye as he gleefully needled her. She could see that her old friend had not changed.

"Brian, number one—drop the Maggie May, it's Margaret. And number two, we will talk about anything you want at breakfast—sports, politics, sex, whatever you want. Goodnight, Brian." With that said, Margaret gave Brian a coquettish smile, and disappeared behind the door to the fifties room. A grin broke out on Brian's face at the sound of the lock clicking behind the door.

"Goodnight, Maggie May," he whispered in a voice too low for her to hear. Margaret sat down on the bed and listened to Brian's steps descend the stairs. Her reunion with him had played out better than she had expected. Looking across the room, she focused on the picture of Marilyn Monroe. The starlet's picture reminded Margaret that she felt pretty, partly due to the way Brian looked at her after all this time. She shifted her eyes to the portrait of General Eisenhower. Mom had always said that the sight of Dwight Eisenhower made her feel safe and secure. At this moment and for the first time, Margaret fully understood what her mother had tried to convey to her.

* * *

Margaret was lying awake in bed the next morning when three gentle raps were applied on the door to her room.

"Yes, who is it?" she sang out.

"I've brought you up a cup of coffee in your own Atlantic Coast Lodge mug, *Ms.* Olson."

"My own Atlantic Coast Lodge mug? Wow! Suddenly this trip to Maine is beginning to seem worthwhile," she replied. Margaret was not about to let her old friend needle her without giving it right back.

"Don't get too juiced up over the mug. The $4.95 retail value of this exquisite vessel is being added to your tab, even as we speak.

Oh—do you plan on opening the door sometime this morning, Ms. Olson?" called out Brian.

"I'll open it, if you give me three or four seconds to get back under the covers." Margaret jumped down onto the hardwood floor, unlocked the door and slid back between the sheets, as Brian paused a few moments before pushing his way in with a coffee tray in hand. He placed the tray down on the night table to the left of Margaret, and promptly sat on the edge of the bed.

"I take my coffee light with no sugar," she blurted out in a humorously bossy manner. Brian nodded his head and dutifully poured her coffee. He added a generous amount of half and half before stirring the steaming, hot beverage. Then he carefully handed it to her, taking extra precaution not to spill any of the contents. He had a tender look on his face as he stared at his guest.

"Jesus, Keogh, you're in the lodge less than twenty-four hours, and I'm already in the sack with you!" Margaret's mouth was full of coffee so she could not immediately respond. "We'll keep this our little secret," said Brian playfully. He raised himself from the edge of the bed as Margaret stared at him with widened eyes. She was still unable to respond.

"How about this. Why don't you meet me downstairs in forty-five minutes, and I'll spring for breakfast down in Ogunquit." Before Margaret could utter a word, Brian had closed the door behind him and was bounding down the stairs.

An hour after Brian had left her room, Margaret descended the stairs and found her old friend giving instructions to a young, sandy-haired fellow whom he introduced to her as Hal. At the conclusion of his discussion with Hal, Brian turned back to Margaret.

"Who's car, yours or mine?" he asked.

"What do you drive?" questioned Margaret, sounding a little uppity.

"A Ford pickup—and we'll have to pick a few things up from the front seat if we plan on using it." Margaret rolled her eyes and broke out in a frown.

"Why don't we just take my car?" she offered.

Brian nodded, indicating this did not present a problem for him, and they both made their way out to her BMW. Margaret became aware that Brian was closely surveying her as she glanced at herself in the rear view mirror. She had had a good night's sleep and she thought that it showed in her face. This pleased her.

"You'll take a left onto Route 1 at the end of the driveway," instructed Brian. She gave him a fleeting glance and returned her eyes to the road.

"Did you have any problem getting the day off on such short notice?" she asked.

"Not at all. Hal's been haunting me to give him more hours, so this worked out great."

"I was thinking more about the owner, or do you pretty much have the authority to do as you please?" She was concerned that Brian might be jeopardizing his job in some way.

"No problem, Maggie. The guy who owns the complex is one of the finest human beings on earth. Intelligent, good looking, athletic—hell, I could go on and on, but what would be the point?" Brian spoke with a twinkle in his eye, telegraphing the fact he was having some fun at Margaret's expense. She gave a thoughtful sideways glance, but did not respond.

"The man who owns the lodge is—is—well, so much more than a man," he continued as Margaret snuck another quick glance at her passenger.

"You're not saying that you own the lodge, are you?" She asked in disbelief. Her expression caused Brian to laugh out loud.

"I'm one of three owners. I own a third of the stock. We're a corporation, an 'S' corporation. Do you know what that is Maggie—an 'S' corporation?" Brian was intentionally trying to get under her skin.

"No, Brian, I'm the world's stupidest certified public accountant. I have no idea what you're talking about, but I'm really excited at the thought of learning from you. Perhaps I can just sit at your feet, and soak up all of your knowledge?" She was giving it back to him as quickly as he could dish it out. Margaret glanced to her right and again caught Brian staring at her. She was getting the impression that he was enjoying her company.

"You know Keogh, you're not half bad looking for a woman of forty-four," quipped Brian.

"You know damn well I'm thirty-four, smart ass," exploded Margaret. Brian was intentionally keeping the banter going to avoid any prolonged periods of silence. He had not spent enough time with his old friend to mend the cracks that seventeen years had put in their relationship.

"We're in Ogunquit and we have to make a decision. Do you want a great breakfast in the village, or shall we go to Perkin's Cove to a place with an ocean view? If we dine in the village you'll be able to eat with the locals," added Brian sarcastically.

"Eating with one local is more than enough if you don't mind. Which one will cost you more?" she chided.

"Perkin's Cove," he answered.

"Then it's Perkin's Cove," she replied. Brian laughed and directed her to take a left turn at the town's main intersection in the village. Following an oblique left turn, they motored along a narrow street, bordered on both sides by an assortment of boutiques, travel lodges, art studios, and luxury condominium buildings. Without question, Ogunquit was pleasing to the eye. It was a nice place to be with an old friend. The car was silent for almost a minute before Margaret spoke up.

"You know, Brian, I'm more than a little impressed with you owning a piece of the lodge."

"I was in the right place at the right time. A couple of guys with money to invest let me in on the purchase of the complex with a smaller cash investment. I, however, provided the expertise in running the place."

Brian directed Margaret into a parking lot on a grassy rise overlooking a small, quaint inlet that she would soon learn was Perkin's Cove. She stopped and admired the pristine setting of this small body of water as they got out of the car and walked toward the restaurant. Margaret observed that this location, too, had an assortment of craft shops, art galleries, and condos. A narrow footbridge extended across the small body of water.

"It's a drawbridge for foot traffic," injected Brian.

"It's a wonderful spot," she said as they entered the restaurant.

They were seated at a window table overlooking the cove, and handed menus by a tall, drawn-looking waitress. After briefly reviewing the menu Brian reopened their conversation.

"So, Keogh, you already know I'm single. What's the story with you?" There was nothing threatening in his voice.

"Well—in a manner of speaking, I'm married."

"In a manner of speaking. What manner of speaking is that, Maggie?" Brian now spoke with a quiet earnestness.

"Okay, Brian, you make the call. My husband moved out of the house in January and has not set foot in it since. He's living with a girl who appears to be just a few years older than my daughter. We talk on the phone for five minutes or so every couple of weeks. So, you make the call. Am I married?" Brian picked up on some bitterness in her voice, in spite of her efforts to mask it.

"In a manner of speaking," he replied apologetically.

Suddenly, there came the sound of crashing china and glassware on the floor. The waitress had just passed by their table. From her vantage point, Margaret watched the accident unfold. Their waitress had lost control of the tray destined for the table of an elderly couple a few feet away. A startled outcry came from the silver-haired woman for whom the meal was intended. The startled howls were soon replaced by a volley of harsh criticisms, mostly directed at the unfortunate waitress. For her part, the waitress stood motionless over the scrambled remains of two breakfasts. Brian turned to see the elderly couple reaching for their coats, angrily making their way to the door. The waitress remained perfectly still for what seemed like a full thirty seconds, her back to Margaret and Brian. Finally, the woman slowly knelt down and methodically began placing the plates and glasses back onto her tray.

"Nice place you brought me to," whispered Margaret, trying to lighten the mood.

"That's got to be embarrassing," said Brian, not picking up on Margaret's attempt to shift their attention away from the mishap. He glanced back to the scene of the commotion and watched as the manager pulled the waitress aside, presumably to lecture her for the blunder. Brian trained his eyes on the two.

"Excuse me for a second, Maggie. I'll be right back." With this said, Brian rose to his feet and walked across the room to where the manager and waitress were conversing. Seconds later, Margaret watched as Brian joined the two and began speaking directly to the young man in charge. He spoke for no more than a minute. Finally, Brian shook the manager's hand, touched the waitress on the forearm, and returned to Margaret at the table.

"What the hell was that all about?" she asked, totally bewildered.

"I told the guy that I may have been responsible for the accident."

"Were you?" asked a puzzled Margaret.

"No."

"Then why did you say you were?"

"I felt sort of sorry for her. I mean, God, she's got this boss, who's probably young enough to be her son, climbing all over her in the corner. I just felt sorry for her." Brian glanced intermittently out the window as he spoke, causing Margaret to question his sincerity.

"Did you see her face when she was at our table? She looks like she's had a tough time of it. She looks like she could use a break," he continued.

"I don't get it! Does she turn you on or something?" said Margaret accusingly. Margaret had turned serious. "I'd hate to think you're trying to score points with another woman while you're with me."

"Will you relax?" said Brian. "Stop being such a little hothead! God—you've always had such a short fuse. Trust me, since I found you in my parlor last night, you have had my undivided attention. I just felt sorry for her. The woman looked like she could use a break!" Brian now seemed sincere, and Margaret thought she heard the first hint of flirtation in his words. She took a deep breath and forced herself to calm down.

"That's the only reason? You felt sorry for her?"

"Maybe one more. Now this is going to sound nuts, but when the last judgment comes, I'm going to be a close call. I could go either way. Something like this could put me over the top—allow me to slither in. The Big Guy's going to remind me of the day I took a gorgeous CPA to breakfast and maybe saved some poor waitress's job. Then He'll say—Kelly, that moronic stunt you pulled in Ogunquit back in 1991—that thing with the waitress and the food on the floor, well, it put you over the top. So Kelly, why don't you just slide on in here with all these saints and all." Brian took a sip of coffee and watched for his friend's reaction.

"Brian, you are just as weird as you were back in school." Margaret's tone let him know that her anger was subsiding.

"There is a downside to all this though. I offered to pay for the two meals that wound up on the floor, and junior's going to take me up on it. Maybe my rich friend from New Hampshire can help me with the check?" asked Brian, kiddingly.

"Bullshit! As a matter of fact, I've decided to order eggs Benedict— the terribly overpriced eggs Benedict. This breakfast is going to set you back a few bucks." Margaret chuckled as she spoke, letting Brian know that she was over her tantrum.

During the meal, the beleaguered waitress made a point to thank Brian for his gesture of kindness. She followed this with an offer to reimburse him. Brian balked at being repaid. By the end of breakfast even Margaret was speaking to the waitress as if she were an old acquaintance. Following breakfast, Margaret and Brian walked directly back to the car. Reaching the BMW, he reached out his hand.

"Friends?" He extended his hand for a few seconds before Margaret reached over and slipped her fingers through his.

"Best friends," she answered.

The two decided to take a drive south following their hearty meal. Brian directed Margaret to turn the car onto a winding coastal road that started them toward York. Margaret was first to speak.

"Brian, forgive me for bringing up business, but how happy are you with your accountant?"

"He gets the job done. Plus, he's sort of the submissive type, just like you." Brian hoped to get a rise out of Margaret, but did not.

"He's marginally better looking than you, too. Why do you ask? What are you getting at, Maggie May?"

"I'll let that Maggie May business pass for now. I was just wondering if you would be interested in letting me know what you need in the way of financial and tax services. Perhaps I could prepare a proposal on having my firm bid on the work, the next time you decide to do some comparative shopping."

"Who would do the actual work at your end? You, or one of your flunkies?" needled Brian.

"Well, first of all, I don't hire flunkies. But, to answer your question, I would probably do the majority of the work myself, at least for the first year anyway." Margaret glanced across the front seat of the car and caught Brian admiring her legs.

"Do you have any business cards with you?" he asked.

"Check the glove compartment."

He opened the compartment and sifted through an assortment of items stored there. Brian sighed audibly a couple of times as he rummaged over a number of Margaret's cosmetic articles.

"I don't see any," he finally scoffed.

"Open your eyes, Kelly. Look for a small plastic bag. They've got to be there." Brian resumed shuffling the contents of the compartment and finally pulled something out.

"You keep your business cards in a plastic sandwich bag?" Brian made the statement as if in disbelief. "She keeps her business cards in a plastic sandwich bag," he repeated. She glared across the front seat of the car at him.

"It keeps them clean and the edges stay sharp," said Margaret defensively. Margaret glanced back at Brian, catching him rolling his eyes. She expected a sarcastic comment from him, but he decided not to respond.

After arriving in York, Brian directed Margaret onto a road that paralleled a high cliff. This gave them a panoramic view of the open ocean from the right side of the car. They drove for about a mile before pulling into a circular parking lot at land's end. To their right and left was the sparkling blue water of the Atlantic. Straight ahead, at the eastern tip of this spit of land was Nubble Light, a picturesque lighthouse built on a little island no more than forty yards offshore.

"Oh God, I've seen this spot in pictures a million times!" exclaimed Margaret.

The couple got out of the car and strolled to the edge of the rock formation facing Nubble Light. In addition to the lighthouse, the tiny island had a single family house that must have been home to the lighthouse keeper and his family at one time. A chilly breeze was blowing in from the north, prompting Margaret to fold her arms and give off a shivering sound. Reaching around her shoulder, Brian pulled her next to him. There was a degree of tenderness in his manner. Margaret neither spoke nor resisted. It made her feel warmer.

"If you're cold we can get back in the car," he offered.

"No, just a few minutes more. This is a wonderful spot. Do you come here often?"

"A few times a year anyway. It's ten or fifteen miles from Wells, so it's not always convenient. There are usually scuba divers on the north side over here, but I don't see any sign of them today." Brian spun her around and faced her northward. Finally, Margaret had withstood as much of the north wind as she could, and the two returned to the car. On the trip back to Wells they decided to return to the lodge, fill a thermos with hot cocoa, and visit Parson's Beach.

Following a twenty-minute stop at the Atlantic Coast Lodge, the couple tossed the thermos of cocoa into the BMW, and sped north toward Parson's Beach. Margaret instructed Brian that she did not want any assistance finding the beach, and proceeded to locate the entrance road with little difficulty. Slowly, she drove up the narrow, tree-lined country road. It was the road they traveled together so many years before. A rush of nostalgia washed over her as the BMW crawled over the small bridge, lifting them over the narrow neck of water at the entrance to the parking lot.

"Well, I guess we're finally back," announced Margaret.

"No one's going to accuse us of being in a rut, that's for sure," retorted Brian.

They exited the car, the only one in the lot, and walked toward the beach. Brian took Margaret's hand, then gently squeezed it as they stopped and looked down the length of the shoreline.

"Maggie, it's hard to believe, but an entire decade, the eighties, has come and gone since we were together here. I mean—think of it! Ronald Reagan's entire presidency came and went. Don't you find it unbelievable?"

"Unbelievable and sad—almost too sad to think about," answered Margaret in a tone that reflected her now-thoughtful mood.

"Why don't we head south, like we did last time we were here?" suggested Brian. Margaret nodded in agreement and the two proceeded to walk slowly beside the crashing surf. A minute or two later, she broke the silence.

"Did you ever feel funny about bringing me here back then? You know, with my being so big and all?"

"Not really. I figured people thought we were a young married couple or something. I know I wasn't self-conscious or anything." Margaret was thinking how enjoyable it was speaking to Brian, particularly when he remained serious.

"But God, Brian, we must have looked so young!" she exclaimed.

"Well, you asked me a question, and I gave you an honest answer. Besides, you were a cute, little blimp when you were pregnant. I'll bet a lot of guys were jealous of me last time we were here," he said.

Margaret let out a howl, then started to laugh. She stared down at the sand in front of them as they continued to walk. Looking up, Margaret saw that Brian was staring at her, the way someone would stare at a painting or sculpture, she thought. There was no doubt in her mind anymore, Brian Kelly was enjoying her company.

There was a momentary lull in the conversation during which Brian awkwardly bumped against Margaret while continuing to stroll beside her. She remained silent, knowing his clumsiness was intentional. It was she who broke a prolonged silence. "Can you accept a little constructive criticism?"

Brian forced a pained expression. "If I say I cannot, will I be spared your criticism?"

"No, and what's more you'll expose yet another of your many character flaws," chided Margaret. Brian stared over at his friend for a moment before gesturing her to continue.

"Back at the lodge this morning, just before we left for breakfast—you were giving that kid instructions. I couldn't help but overhear the conversation. You were treating the whole matter like it was management by committee. He was asking why this and why that! I mean the way you explained every little thing to him seemed to be a bit much." Margaret's voice contained a hint of loftiness.

"And how do they do things back at the Maggie May Keogh School of Business Management?" smirked Brian.

Margaret did not miss a beat. "There is no more efficient form of government or leadership than that of a benevolent dictatorship! Decisions are made at the top—by one leader—and carried out by the rest of the organization. I don't want to feel obliged to explain my every decision to each and every soldier in my army. Do you see where I'm coming from, Brian?" she asked. Brian looked over to Margaret with an exaggerated look of confusion.

"I'm lost," he answered.

"What can't you follow?" fired back Margaret, impatiently.

"Oh, I get the part about the dictatorship and how things are done in your office. It's the thing about you and a benevolent dictatorship that's hanging me up. Somehow Maggie Keogh and benevolence is just a little hard to swallow." Margaret shot Brian a sideward glance, her eyes narrowed into mere slits. This was the facial expression she would use back at the office to express nonverbal displeasure with an employee. It did not have the same effect on Brian that it had on a staff member whose employment status Margaret had absolute control over. She turned and delivered a friendly punch to Brian's shoulder. Brian took it as her way of dropping the subject.

"By the way Brian, how did we leave that matter of whether or not I could put a proposal together on the accounting and tax work for Atlantic Coast Lodge?"

"I believe I was being noncommittal on the matter, when you brought it up back in Ogunquit." Brian was speaking slowly, as if running something over in his mind.

"Well, make a decision. You claim to be a businessman—make a decision," shot back Margaret. There was an aggressive edge in her voice. He stared at her for a moment. Margaret sensed that Brian was contemplating something before springing it on her.

"Well?" She was pushing the matter now, giving him no escape route.

"Tell you what, Keogh—if you let me give you a relaxing massage sometime before you leave, I'll give you a shot at the corporation's tax work." Brian stared straight ahead as he delivered his proposition. A bewildered look came over Margaret's face as she contemplated Brian's words.

"You want a massage from me?" she asked, seemingly confused.

"No, Keogh, you're not listening. You let me give you the massage and I give you a crack at the tax work." Brian spoke deliberately, overemphasizing each word. "Massage is sort of my hobby. I've read a thousand books on it and I think I'm pretty good at it."

A smile broke across Margaret's face. It was one of those "I've got you figured out" smiles. "By any chance, you wouldn't be thinking that you'd be getting me all hot and bothered by your massage strokes, and ripe for seduction, would you?"

"Oh, don't we think a lot of ourselves," said Brian sarcastically. "I can't blame you for hesitating. You're a long way from home. I'm practically a stranger. I could be some deranged pervert for all you know. Maggie, I'm sorry if I offended you."

"Brian, I'm not offended, but you're dealing with the original ice princess here. All you'd get from me is frustrated," Margaret laughingly explained.

"I can deal with a little frustration," quipped Brian, his voice trailing off as he spoke. Margaret looked up and met his eyes.

"Then you're on." Neither one added anything to the agreement, but instead decided to leave it as stated. They continued to walk southward. Little had changed along this stretch of shoreline since 1973. Margaret attempted to locate the rock they had sat on together years before. She remembered distinctly how it was shaped, almost like a chair. She was disappointed that they could not locate it now. Eventually, Margaret turned the conversation back to more personal topics.

"So, Brian, I've given you some insight into my personal life, pathetic as it is. How about you? There must be someone with their hooks in you, even if you're not married yet?"

Brian looked to the heavens and smiled. He realized that Margaret had been quite candid with him, and now he should return the favor.

"Quite a few years ago, there was someone who was very special. It wasn't meant to be though. God, it's been almost ten years. Right now there is a woman I see quite a bit of—when she's home." Brian was guarding his words, which Margaret picked up on right away.

"Oh, when she's home? Her job puts her on the road a lot?"

"No Maggie, it's not her job. She's away at school at the moment," stated Brian sheepishly.

"School! She's away at school! Pray tell, is she at least a senior?" asked Margaret. "You know Brian, if you'd like, I could give you my daughter Jenny's phone number. She'll be in college this coming September." Margaret was laughing as she spoke.

"Okay, Maggie May, let me know when you're through. I wouldn't want to spoil your fun. When you're through, I'll fill you in on all the juicy details. I'll put it in perspective." Brian spoke kiddingly. He did not seem agitated in spite of the onslaught from his friend.

Margaret reached over and pulled his head down, kissing him on the cheek. Following this gesture, she gave Brian a nod, indicating she was ready for his explanation.

"Molly is a twenty-two-year-old sophomore at the University of Vermont. She took a couple of years off after high school to travel.

Most folks around here use the word "eccentric" to describe her. She is very bright, reasonably attractive, and a free spirit. So, you see, the age difference isn't all that bad—about twelve or thirteen years," concluded Brian.

"Hmmm, twelve years you say. Let's see—twelve years," repeated Margaret. "So Brian, that means when you were a freshman in college, little Molly was clapping erasers in Miss Crabtree's first grade class—and probably still wetting her bed. Yes, I think that does put things in perspective." Margaret giggled as she spoke while staring coyly at Brian out of the corner of her eye.

"You know, Keogh, you're actually kind of cute when you act like this, in a sadistic sort of way." Margaret responded by innocently throwing her arms around Brian, resulting in a prolonged, mutual embrace. Finally, following twenty seconds of silence, Margaret initiated a physical separation.

"So, are you going to tell little Molly about me?" she asked sarcastically.

"That depends on if there's anything to tell. After all, if you are the ice princess, all there will be are stories about our walks on the beach, and trips down memory lane. She might find that a little boring."

Margaret stared at him, a thoughtful look covered her face. She chose not to respond to his statement. They spent over an hour walking the length of Parson's Beach. From there, they drove north on Route 1 to Portland, where Brian guided Margaret through the art galleries and specialty shops of the waterfront district. They were becoming more and more relaxed with each other with each passing hour. Margaret and Brian spent time filling in the blanks that made up the years of their lives from high school on through adulthood. Brian was candid about personal matters, including lost loves and his limited educational background. For her part, Margaret spoke sparingly about the personal details in her life. She talked about Jenny, but little of Brad. She knew it would make her uncomfortable speaking of him, and she was not sure how Brian would react to having the discussion focused on another man. Eventually, Margaret had the conversation centered on her accounting practice, and the recent restoration work done on the office building in Manchester. To her delight, Brian displayed a genuine interest in her professional career. This pleased her. There was nothing Margaret enjoyed speaking about more than herself.

At her insistence, they dined in a restaurant on the pier overlooking Portland Harbor. She chided Brian for not ordering seafood, and for nursing a single beer throughout the course of their meal. For her part, Margaret ordered several of the bartender's specialty, Singapore slings, despite warnings from Brian. She responded by questioning his authenticity as a true Irishman. Over the next hour, she managed to make a real mess of her twin lobster dinner, while Brian displayed a higher degree of civility on his chicken cordon bleu. Diplomatically, and with great effort, Brian was able to limit Margaret to three drinks.

Following dinner, Margaret was talkative and more free-spirited on the drive back to Wells. Brian offered to drive, and Margaret agreed without an argument. She fastened herself into the passenger seat of her car and stared across at her old friend at length. She could see a hint of gray hair beginning to show at his temples, but still, the passage of time was being kind to him. The faint wrinkles beginning to form around his eyes gave his face a distinguished character. Margaret thought how Brian was not a handsome man by the world's standards, but he was a physically attractive one. Then, the alcohol in her system set her to chattering.

"Brian, will you be completely honest with me about something?" she asked.

"Absolutely, fire away."

"Am I a beautiful woman? No bullshit now, I want the truth." The question let Brian know that the three drinks Margaret had gulped down back in Portland were kicking in.

"Well, Maggie, for starters, you're body is a ten, hands down. You must have to work like hell to look the way you do." He glanced over, catching her eye.

"You'll never know what I have to go through to stay in this kind of condition. I didn't ask you that! I know my body is a ten! But—am I beautiful? How would you rate me? One to ten." She seemed seriously concerned.

"Uhhhh—in all honesty, between an eight and a nine," he stated emphatically.

"How can you say that!" Margaret exploded. "So that means if you walk in a room where there are ten randomly picked women, there will be two who are more beautiful than me? That's what you're saying?"

"Oh, man, how did I let you sucker me into this conversation? First of all, there is nothing wrong with being an eight! Hell, most men would die for women who are eights," he remarked.

"Would you die for me Brian, seeing that I'm an eight and all?" Margaret asked pathetically.

"Well, to be completely honest Keogh, I have this hard and fast rule. I don't lay down my life for anything less than a ten, and you just don't cut it." Brian needled his old friend while shooting admiring glances across to her side of the car.

"Okay Kelly, how about me telling you what I think you are—numerically I mean?" she asked in a playful snarl.

"Not interested—just not interested," he responded. Then, before Margaret could tag him with a numerical rating, Brian shifted the conversation to a new topic.

"Maggie, out of curiosity, what nationality are you?"

"I'm English and Scottish. Why?"

"English and Scottish—cold and cheap." Brian laughed as he tried to get a rise out of her.

"Cold, cheap and ugly. I'm only an eight," moaned Margaret. Brian reached over and draped his right arm around her, pulling her closer to him. She rested her head on his shoulder.

"You know, a lot of men are intimidated by me," commented Margaret soberly. The topic of conversation had taken another ninety-degree turn.

"That's quite a revelation Maggie May. What could men possibly find intimidating about an overambitious, overly critical, demanding, materialistic, opinionated, highly successful businesswoman—even if she happens to be disarmingly sexy and brilliant?" Brian was speaking in a sarcastic tone.

"Nice recovery! You're absolutely right, Brian. You see, that's what I like about you. You were quick to recognize that you're my inferior and you accept it at that." She spoke with her head still resting on his shoulder. "Now, how is this going to work? Are we going to the lodge and up to my room—for the massage I mean?"

Brian's stomach knotted in reaction to her question. "I was thinking more like going down to my cottage at the beach, you know, for the privacy," he whispered.

"Whoa, house at the beach! You never told me you had a beach house. I figured you lived at the lodge," replied Margaret excitedly.

"Wait a minute, Maggie May. You said a house at the beach, not me! I said 'cottage at the beach.' There's a difference."

"God, Brian, this is exciting. You're a man of surprises!"

"Wait a minute Keogh. Before you get your materialistic little hopes up, let me return you to planet Earth. We're not talking about some fifteen-room house with crashing surf at the front door. I have a small—and the operative word here is small—cottage, about a hundred yards from the beach. But it is special. It's at the end of a private, dead-end street, and the water from the estuary comes right up to the edge of the property. It gives me an unobstructed view of the estuary and wildlife sanctuary," said Brian proudly.

"Now, do you own this yourself?" quizzed Margaret.

"Me and the Kennebunk Savings Bank," he said in his typically humble manner.

"Do you keep it clean?" scoffed Margaret.

"Well, Ms. Keogh, let's just say it's clean enough for some little hick houseguest from New Hampshire. It's not like you're some conti-nent- hopping jet-setter. You're a humble bookkeeper from New Hamp-shire," jested Brian. Still influenced by her Singapore slings, Margaret decided to play along with him. She dropped her eyes and pouted. The pout made her appear juvenile. It brought a smile to Brian's face.

"You don't think I'm pretty enough to be a jet-set girl and, on top of that, you think I'm just a bookkeeper." Margaret was being unchar-acteristically silly. Brian enjoyed seeing his friend in this mood. He turned halfway serious for a moment.

"You are plenty pretty enough, and if you were anything like those people you wouldn't even be getting a massage from me tonight."

9

BACK IN WELLS Brian made a quick stop at a local convenience store. He hopped out of the car without saying a word and minutes later emerged from the store with a plastic bottle in his hand. Climbing back into the driver's seat, he flipped the bottle into Margaret's lap. She gazed down to see it was baby oil. She looked over at him.

"I take it this is for the massage."

"This will allow my hands to literally glide over even those parts of your body with the driest of skin. For all I know, I could be facing skin like bleached horse hide," he added.

"Thanks for the vote of confidence," retorted Margaret.

Brian turned the BMW down Mile Road directly toward the Atlantic. About one hundred yards ahead of the beach parking lot, he took a right turn onto a roadway that roughly paralleled the coastline and, less than a minute later, he turned the car onto a private, dead-end street. The sun was setting behind the distant tree line across the marshland, accentuating a blue ribbon of estuary water at the end of the street. The car slowly rolled to a stop in front of a modest, yellow cottage at the end of the road.

"Is this it?" she asked excitedly. Brian nodded yes.

"I love it!" blurted out Margaret as she took Brian's hand and began pulling him toward the front door. She pulled him up onto an expansive wooden deck that wrapped around the building in an L-shape. She opened the front door onto a small screened porch, large enough only for a compact table for two and a sofa. On the plus side, the porch did offer an unobstructed, 180-degree view of the marshland and wildlife sanctuary. Margaret tried the front door with no success and turned to Brian for assistance.

"Don't expect too much," he said, fumbling in his pocket trying to locate his key chain. Seconds later Brian produced the key and unlocked the door. Margaret jumped ahead of him into a simply decorated, yet meticulously clean, combination living room and dining room.

"Oh God, it's so you, Brian," she exclaimed.

"Well, it's a man's place. I'm not going to have throw pillows and doilies and crap like that." Brian sounded a little defensive.

"I think it's wonderful, I really do." She approached him and squeezed his arm. Then Margaret walked over to the thermostat.

"Do you mind?" Brian nodded his approval and Margaret turned the electric heat on. Somehow she sensed that it meant a great deal to Brian for the cottage to meet with her approval. Opening the door behind him, Brian revealed a compact but fully equipped kitchen. Margaret scanned the small room in amazement. Although sparkling clean and orderly, the appliances and furnishings were dated. The kitchen was dominated by a creamy white Frigidaire refrigerator complete with the chrome handle popularized in the late fifties. Above it was a green, Art Deco clock, the likes of which Margaret had not seen years, maybe decades. Glancing to her left, she spotted an array of small kitchen utensils dangling from a metal rack. Among the utensils was a red-handled potato masher. Margaret could not contain her amusement.

"Damn it, Brian, have I just stepped into a time slip or something? What the hell year are you living in?" Margaret asked through controlled laughter.

"Listen, Keogh, it all works so I see no point in throwing it out," answered Brian defensively.

"Is this a gag or something?" Margaret asked in amusement. She was pointing at a glass orange-squeezer sitting between a dated set of salt and pepper shakers.

"I wouldn't have my orange juice prepared any other way," Brian retorted. Margaret let out a condescending moan and continued on her inspection. Running her finger along the window, she was amazed to come up with not even a hint of dust.

"Any chance of you coming home with me for the day and getting my kitchen looking like this?" she jested. Brian laughed at her back-handed compliment and moved through toward the next room. Turning the iron, antique latch, Margaret swung the door open into a bedroom walled in knotty pine.

"I love knotty pine," whispered Margaret wistfully. "There's something about it that's so restful to the eye. You know, I actually know of some people back home who have whitewashed over it. Do you believe it! Somehow I can't imagine you doing something like that." Margaret was speaking to Brian warmly. Her words were not necessarily warm, but her tone and manner was. She sat down on the edge of the bed and looked up at him coyly.

"So, is this where I'm going to get my long, luxurious massage—and earn myself a new client?"

"Dammit, Keogh, you already have me signing the dotted line. Give me a break! But to answer your question, yes, this is where you'll get the most exhilarating massage of your drab, pathetic life." Margaret responded with a giggle as she picked up on what she perceived to be the first evidence of nervousness in Brian.

"So Brian, how does this work? Do I just undress down to my undergarments and let you take it from there? I've never received a massage from anyone but my husband and maybe a lover back in college. You're going to have to talk me through this."

Brian stepped across the room to the doorway leading to the bathroom. Reaching around the corner, he produced two white, fluffy towels. He tossed them onto the bed next to her.

"Tell you what, Keogh. I'll pour us a couple of glasses of punch and allow you to get undressed in privacy. When I come back from the kitchen, why don't you have yourself lying in the middle of the bed with one towel over your breasts and the other over your midsection." Margaret was now grinning sheepishly.

"What part of me do you plan on massaging first, Brian?" she asked coyly.

"Your face," he replied instantly.

"My face!" she exclaimed.

"I have my own technique. For example, right now I'm looking at a little tightass—alluring—but still a tightass, and the first thing I know I have to do is relax those facial muscles. Once the muscles around your eyes and mouth have relaxed, I'll move to your feet. Now we're talking pleasure almost beyond your wildest dreams. Think of it, Keogh—countless nerve endings and my talented hands rubbing and bending your feet until it feels like your whole body is suspended in midair. If you're a good subject, I may even toss in a short lecture on reflexology, the art of relieving pain through foot massage." Brian was speaking playfully, indicating to Margaret that he was beginning to relax.

"Jesus, Brian, this is really beginning to sound wonderful. I'm already considering how much to tip you when it's over."

"Don't insult me, Maggie. I'm an artist when it comes to massage. I don't want to hear any of your monetary bullshit brought into it," retorted Brian, pretending to be insulted.

"Well, when you start referring to yourself as an artist, bullshit automatically comes to mind." Margaret responded immediately and effortlessly. Her words had them chuckling for a few seconds.

"That's absolutely the last straight line you get from me tonight, Keogh," snarled Brian.

"We'll see," she countered. Brian jumped to his feet.

"Okay, Maggie, I'm going to the kitchen to get us something to sip on. Why don't you change in here and get yourself set up."

Margaret nodded in the affirmative and Brian stepped out into the kitchen. As she removed her skirt and blouse Margaret made a point of hanging them in the room's open closet. She paused for a moment, deliberating where to place her undergarments, then opted to place them on the floor at the far side of the bed.

"What do I do with my necklace?" she called out.

"Only an accountant would have to ask that question," hollered Brian in return.

She took Brian's sarcasm to mean that the necklace should come off, so she cautiously opened the hinge and dropped it on the oak bureau to the right of the bed. Margaret then positioned herself in the center of the bed. She draped one totally unfolded towel over her mid-section. The second towel she placed over her breasts, folded in half. Margaret was not what the women's magazines described as generously endowed. This had never bothered her and she was bewildered by other women who lamented any deficiency in this area. The important thing was that the towels covered her adequately. From the living room came the faint sound of classical music.

"How did you know I liked classical music?" she called out.

"Some things you just know," said Brian. "Besides, it goes well with a massage," he answered.

Brian eased open the door with his shoulder, a glass of juice in each hand, and looked down at his friend. It pleased him to see how at ease she looked lying on the bed. Margaret noticed that Brian had changed into sweat pants and a tee shirt.

"I'm glad to see you lying on your back and not your stomach," he commented.

"Well you said you'd be starting with a facial massage didn't you?"

"Yeah, I did, but then again you had to ask about the necklace so I wasn't sure you'd figure it out." Brian seemed totally relaxed by this time. He put the two glasses down on the bureau within reach of the bed and climbed on behind Margaret, nudging her lower down on the mattress. Then, Brian positioned a pillow on his lap and lifted her head, placing it in the center of the pillow.

"Are you comfortable?" he asked.

"Very," she replied.

"All right, Keogh, I want you to blot out everything except the sensation of my hands on your skin. No thoughts about the office back home or how you might overcharge me for your tax services. Remember now, you're with a friend whom you can trust and nothing but relaxation and pleasure will come from all this. Agreed?"

"Agreed," she answered. Margaret was lying with her eyes closed by now.

Brian began running the tips of his fingers lightly across her face and through her hairline. He switched from below to above her eyes then, after a couple of minutes, he began kneading the facial surface between and directly above her eyes.

"You've allowed a certain amount of stress to build up in your facial muscles. I can feel it. If I do my job right, you'll be able to look in the mirror when we're done and see the difference. Now bring your hands up closer to me so I can massage your palms," Brian ordered.

Margaret obliged by assuming a "hands-up" position and Brian proceeded to jiggle the fingers on both hands simultaneously for a few moments. He followed this by rubbing Margaret's palms with his thumbs.

"Why are your hands so slippery?" she asked accusingly.

"Have you forgotten the baby oil I picked up at the store?"

"Oh, that's right. My little Brian picked up baby oil for my massage." Margaret was showing all the signs of total relaxation.

"Wait a minute, Keogh. Why did you think my hands were so slippery?" questioned Brian playfully. Margaret exploded into a howl of laughter, joined by Brian. Over the next few minutes, he continued with the relaxing rub, switching from her hands to her arms and neck. Margaret became aware that the wind had picked up outside and was making a pleasant, whistling sound through the cottage's eaves. Brian was rolling her neck in a circular motion when Margaret broke a five-minute silence.

"This is so wonderful. It really is."

"If you think you're relaxed now, wait'll you see what's in store for you next." Brian withdrew his body from beneath her, letting her head drop back onto the pillow. Then, setting himself up at the bottom of the bed, he took hold of her right foot, propping it up on his folded leg. He began kneading the surface of her foot with his strong hands.

"You have a greater concentration of nerve endings in your feet than anywhere else in your body. Now Maggie, clear your mind of everything except the strokes of my hand over the surface of your skin." Margaret did not say a word, choosing to follow his command without question. Eyes closed, she totally engrossed herself in the feel of Brian's hands. Nothing was said for the next few minutes as Brian manipulated her ankle in a circular motion, then flexed each of her toes individually.

"Please stay with the feet for a while longer," she pleaded. "I am really enjoying this." Her face was carrying a faint smile, telling Brian how much enjoyment he was giving her. She still had her eyes closed.

"Do you know what you do that I really like?" she asked in a relaxed tone.

"No, what?" he asked in a whisper.

"I love it when you call me Keogh. I put up with it when you call me Maggie—and I could kill you when you call me Maggie May—but I love it when you call me Keogh. I guess it makes me feel like a teenager or something."

Margaret glanced up at Brian, catching his eyes focused on her. He was being unusually quiet.

"Five more minutes with the feet and then on to those flabby legs of yours," he said with a chuckle.

"Flabby! I spend twenty minutes a day on my Soloflex to ensure they're not flabby," answered Margaret.

"I was only kidding, Hothead. These legs of yours are anything but flabby. God, your legs look like those girl gymnast's legs at the Olympics," he conceded.

"Well, for that crack about the flabby legs, I want ten extra minutes on the feet. No, make it fifteen," she ordered. Margaret decided to use Brian's good-natured kidding as leverage.

"Okay, ten more—but that's it!" he said.

Margaret lowered her head back on the pillow and returned to a state of pure, physical enjoyment. She began to contemplate how wonderful it was being at the coast and away from the office. She thought she heard the sound of waves crashing a hundred yards away over the wail of the wind. Margaret opened her eyes a slit to watch as Brian continued to work on her feet. Margaret was taking this time to look at Brian—really look at him. She thought he was more attractive than she had remembered. He seemed to be one of those people who got better looking as they grew older, she thought. He still had the same thick shock of brown hair but his face had changed. It had filled in. Back in high school Brian had been wiry, but now he was solid, although still on the lean side. Margaret was suddenly aware that she was attracted to him. For the first time, it struck her that something sexual could develop between them this evening. Margaret realized that she was in the early stages of sexual arousal. Instantly, she decided to follow her instincts and see what happened. The minutes passed and finally Brian placed her foot back on the mattress.

"Soloflex, huh? Let's see how firm Miss Soloflex's legs are," Brian said. He pretended to examine her legs as if it were the first time he had laid eyes on them. In reality, he had been admiring them since his first opportunity, on the ride to Ogunquit that morning. Following a few more seconds of exaggerated examination, he announced his verdict.

"Not too bad, for a New Hampshire girl." Margaret was about to mount her counterattack when Brian began a deep-rubbing technique on her well-developed calf muscle.

"Tell me if it hurts, Maggie. It shouldn't, but just in case it does. All kidding aside, you have terrific legs. I don't see legs like these up here in Maine except during the tourist season." Margaret let go with a soft, extended sigh.

"God, Brian, you are good at this—damned good."

His rhythmic kneading of her tight calf muscles went on for an indeterminable period, as kept by Margaret's internal clock, when he abruptly shifted his attention up her leg to above the knee. He did this without the fanfare that had accompanied the earlier repositioning of the massage area. Margaret felt his hands on the outside and then the inside of her thighs. Margaret knew his hands were now clearly invading an erogenous zone. Although nothing was being said, Margaret was sure Brian was aware that he was arousing her. She was now taking long, audible breaths as her body began to awaken from its prolonged slumber. His strong hands continued upward under the towel. Margaret's vaginal muscles were involuntarily throbbing at this point. Furthermore, the pleasant scent of her passion was beginning to fill the room.

"God, Brian, I'm getting really wet." She whispered, fearing the spoken word could dissuade him. Margaret felt the towel slip from atop her body, followed by a series of tender kisses progressing up her thigh and into her most erotic region. Seconds later, Brian Kelly was tasting her.

Purposefully, eagerly, longingly, his tongue explored her, sending waves of ecstasy through her body. His technique was new and welcomed. With pleasure washing over her, Margaret blocked everything but Brian out of her mind. Reaching down, she ran her fingers through his hair. She did not dare speak but she wanted Brian to know the pleasure he was providing her. His hands were under the towel covering her breasts, his fingers flicking and then running tight circles around her hardened nipples.

Over the next few minutes, Brian's tongue continued to strike its erotic target again and again. Margaret's passion continued to heighten until she found herself approaching the point where pleasure and pain converge. At that moment Brian instinctively pulled himself higher onto her and ran his moist tongue over her nipples until his mouth found hers. Another wave of passion enveloped Margaret as she tasted both traces of Brian and herself as his mouth covered hers. Then, he was inside her, the full extent of sexual contact. He held the back of her head in cupped hands as she pulled uncontrollably at his dark hair. This shared passionate intensity went on for what was a split second, or perhaps it was a lifetime, until she cried out. Seconds later, Margaret surrendered to her body's biological mandate. Their bodies thrashed together as Margaret called out Brian's name again and again. Having purged her body of its marvelous demons, Margaret kept her legs locked around Brian. Then, as Margaret arched herself under his rigidly poised body, Brian spent his few fleeting moments of total, sexual ecstasy. A moment later, he slumped down into Margaret's arms. Their moist bodies remained entwined. It occurred to Margaret that, at this precise moment, she and Brian were as close to being one as possible.

"Making love is not always that fantastic for me," said Brian humbly. Perspiration covered both their bodies as they remained in an embrace. Brian made no effort to separate himself from her. He kept his face flush against Margaret's breast. She decided to bring the two lovers back to earth.

"I can't believe how wet your bed is from all this mischief you've gotten me into here," she remarked.

"Perspiration, baby oil, sexual excretions, it all adds up," responded Brian, slowly emerging from his romantic stupor. Again, there was silence for the next few minutes as each tried to reason how this turn of events could alter their lives. Margaret glanced up at the room's radio/alarm clock on the dresser. The clock read 9:45 P.M. Brian caught her glancing at the clock and checked the time himself.

"Do you realize that twenty-four hours ago I didn't have even the remotest idea that I would ever see you again?" Brian whispered the words directly into her ear.

"Twenty-four hours ago I think I was asleep in one of your parlor chairs. I can't believe how this trip to Maine has gone."

"We've always been friends, Maggie," said Brian.

"But I think we've raised our relationship to a new level, don't you?" Margaret smiled to indicate her agreement. Brian jumped up and brought the two glasses of juice back to bed. They repositioned their naked bodies together on top of the bedsheets. Margaret was now resting her head on Brian's chest.

"This house has a nice feel to it," she observed wistfully.

"What do you mean?" queried Brian.

"I don't know. It just feels inviting or something." Brian did not respond immediately but instead lay there with a smile across his face.

"What's so funny? Does that sound stupid to you?" she asked, thinking that perhaps Brian found her observation foolish.

"Just the opposite, Keogh—I've thought the same thing about this place for a long time. I'm just surprised you could pick up on it in such a short time and with someone else here with you."

"I'm not following you," she said. By now Margaret was leaning her head on one elbow and looking down at Brian, who was still lying next to her.

"Well, it's just that I picked up on the atmosphere in this place from all the time I spent alone here. After a while I became conscious of the positive feel it seemed to have within its walls." Brian noticed that Margaret was listening very attentively and he had a strong desire to explain himself clearly.

"Damn it, how do I explain it? You know how sometimes you can go into a house or a building and you immediately pick up on a certain discomfort level you have. It doesn't have to be a foreboding feeling or anything. You just know something's not right. Well, after living here a while I picked up on the opposite feeling. There was something good and nurturing that I felt within its walls. At first I dismissed it as a fantasy but it kept coming back. It took a while but I eventually came up with what I think is the reason for what I, and now you, have picked up on."

"And what's that?" questioned Margaret.

"When I bought this place it was from an older couple who were moving to Florida to retire. For twenty years they had been renting it out to families as a vacation place. They did it to supplement their income. Now think about it, Maggie—the house is occupied week in and week out every summer by families getting away together at the beach. Fathers and mothers escaping from the bullshit back home and at work—spending some real time with their kids. Enjoying themselves! Kids seeing their parents at play, making terrific memories that they'll keep with them for the rest of their lives. Maybe these parents had to scrimp and save all year to have this special time with their families— and they did it. My theory is that even after they left, a little bit of the joy they experienced stayed behind—trapped within the walls of the cottage. Twenty years of families having good times together and maybe feeling more love than they would back home where all their money problems and other assorted bullshit is all around. Twenty years of this kind of activity can leave something behind. Damn it, if buildings can have ghosts and negative forces in them, then maybe they can have the exact opposite. That's what I think is in this place—an ac- cumulation of good memories and love and warmth. So what do you think Maggie May? Am I nuts?"

Margaret was staring at him with a fond expression radiating through her eyes.

"How did a dumb Irishman with a pathetic associates degree get so smart? And so sexy?" She buried her face into his chest and kissed it tenderly. Margaret was enjoying the security that Brian Kelly and his cottage was providing her from the gusting wind outside.

"Since you brought up the subject of sex and sexiness, is there any chance of you sharing something personal with me?" asked Brian.

"You don't think what we just shared a short while ago was per- sonal?" asked Margaret.

"No, of course I do, Maggie. I just wondered if you'd be willing to confide in me some of your deep secrets?"

"Like what?" she asked suspiciously.

"Oh, like maybe your most exciting fantasy, something like that."

"And if I do share that with you, Brian Kelly—will you, in turn, share your number-one fantasy with me?"

"Absolutely," Brian answered without hesitation. Margaret looked him in the eye for a few seconds before speaking.

"God, I can't believe I'm doing something like this!" she exclaimed. Brian fluffed up his pillow and leaned his head back against the head- board. She could see that he was keenly interested in whatever secrets she might be about to divulge.

"I sometimes fantasize about hiring a young, male accountant—a real hunk—and then breaking all the rules of sexual harassment. Grabbing his ass in the office when no one is looking—assigning him to accompany me on overnight business trips and using my position to make sexual demands of him—and then threatening to ruin his career unless he submits to my demands. I worked at the mall one summer back in college and I had this bastard of a boss, a married guy, who kept trying to make me go down on him at his desk. God, he was a bastard! Well, in my fantasy, I have my young flunky go down on me at my desk. I think it's as much a power trip as a sexual thing. I just know I really enjoy that fantasy. Is that perverted enough for you, Brian?" she asked through a chuckle.

"Christ, I'm going to need a shower after that look into your fantasy world. I hope there's enough soap in the house to clean me off. You are a very sick woman," Brian remarked in jest. "Keogh, I am very disappointed."

"What do you mean, disappointed? It's what you asked for and it's the truth. What more can I tell you?"

"Well, to be completely honest, when you were dumb enough to agree to confide your fantasy in me I thought I'd hear something I could use to render you helpless, sexually I mean. I'd use this information to enslave you—put you totally under my control. I'd get in your blood, I mean really in your blood. But instead of finding out what I need to take charge of this relationship, I get this 'power lunch' bullshit about using men and grabbing their asses. You may be the cutest accountant I've ever laid eyes on but you're really a very sick, troubled, and disturbed woman." Brian's words were light but something in his voice and expression told Margaret that he sincerely cared for her at this moment.

"That may be true, but I'm the sick, troubled, and disturbed woman you have to tell your fantasy to—and right now!" she barked.

Brian jumped from the bed and walked to the bathroom. He was naked and Margaret admired his tight rear end before the door closed behind him. Margaret heard the sound of water running for a few seconds before the door swung open and he stood before her, his arms crossed in front of his chest.

"I'm waiting," she said, not letting him off the hook.

"If you think I'm stupid enough to tell you my fantasy, you're out of your mind," he coolly stated. In a split second Margaret leaped up and grabbed hold of him, dragging him back onto the bed. Brian laughed uncontrollably as Margaret wrestled him down beneath her on the bed. She wore a comical glare on her face as she sat astride her willing victim.

"I'm waiting," she repeated.

Brian tried to catch his breath from the laughter. "Okay, okay—in my fantasy I take a job working for a beautiful, professional woman. I think she's a CPA. She orders me to do all of these kinky things for her at the office. She just won't give me any rest." Brian began to laugh again as Margaret moved herself higher on his chest.

"You are so full of it, Kelly. You expect me to believe that's your fantasy? You get hot thinking about bitchy, female CPAs?"

"Honest, Keogh, I do," he answered. Margaret released her hands from his wrists and slid back down his body. Then, in one motion, she cupped his face with her hands and kissed him purposefully on the lips. Brian reached up to her, pulling her down so that their bodies were aligned.

"Then I'd say we make a perfect pair," she responded.

Margaret remained awake for a time after Brian drifted off to sleep. She thought she heard a distant train whistle carry over the estuary during a short period when the wind temporarily let up. She was thinking about this night with Brian Kelly and her trip up to Maine. Everything about the trip was pleasing her, lifting her spirits. At the moment, it was almost like her problems back in New Hampshire ceased to exist. Margaret glanced down on Brian. It was he who was responsible for making her as happy as she was at this moment. His secret was simple. Brian made her feel like a teenager because in his eyes she was still a teenager. She drew up next to him and listened to him breathe before dropping off to sleep.

10

M ARGARET WAS AWAKENED BY THE SOUND of Brian showering. A quick look at the alarm told her it was 5:15 A.M. She wondered if he was going out to jog at this early hour. She decided to wait until he returned to the room to find out what was happening. A few minutes later he quietly stepped back into the bedroom and began searching for something on the bureau.

"You're not leaving me, are you?" Margaret added a pained, yet comically whining quality to her voice.

"I've got to be at the lodge to open up this morning. Why don't you sleep in and I'll bring you some muffins and coffee later." He planted a soft kiss on her forehead and squeezed her nose between his fingers.

"Thank you for seducing me and then taking advantage of me last night." Margaret delivered her witticism in her best Shirley Temple imitation.

"I'll let that pass. You just be a good girl," he added.

"You, too." Margaret broke out in laughter in response to the look that came over Brian's face.

"Are all the girls back in New Hampshire like you?"

"Yes Brian, we're all quicker and smarter than you, every one of us," she scoffed.

"Quick, smart, and easy to seduce. I like that in women!" He hurriedly shut the door behind him, preventing Margaret from getting in the last word. Seconds later she heard him speed by the window on his bicycle.

Margaret permitted herself the luxury of sleeping late on this particular morning. There was no such thing as sleeping late when tax season was in session. She savored the experience of falling back to sleep time and again. When the desire to rejoin the world finally over-took her, she checked the clock, saw it was just after 9:45 A.M., then pulled herself out of bed. Margaret's first stop was the kitchen, where she saw a half pot of coffee warming on the stove. Brian had put it on for her hours earlier. She felt pampered. It was a small thing but it meant a lot to her. She decided to sit back and wait for him to return. She remembered that he promised to bring her breakfast later in the morning. Margaret was already eagerly anticipating his return, a re-flection of the wonderful time she had the prior evening. In her wild-est dreams Margaret had not allowed herself to anticipate anything as delightful as the past thirty-six hours. She strolled out on the deck and took in the expansive view of the wildlife sanctuary. Then, inexplica-bly, matters from the office managed to slip back into her conscious-ness. Margaret caught herself thinking about Vern Butler. She remem-bered that now he was working out his last two weeks with the firm.

Margaret began to question her decision to dismiss him. Off and on, she had been running the factors over in her mind for a couple of days now. She thought about how much money would be saved by eliminating his salary. By replacing Vern with someone with less ex-perience she could cut the base salary by ten to fifteen thousand dol-lars, minimum. Plus, the new person could be trained to do things more her way. The new person would also be less set in their ways. On the other hand, she would certainly have to expect a drop in perfor-mance. She walked to the far end of the deck and settled herself on a lounge chair as she continued with her internal review of the Vern Butler situation.

Margaret was now considering the circumstances surrounding Vern's dismissal. She had been worn down by the most grueling tax season to date. Her time had been spread to its limit. Then again, Vern had to be by Sarah's side. What was he supposed to do? How much longer would Sarah's treatment go on? A week, maybe two weeks, then what? Margaret stopped to ask herself if it had made sense to discharge her old friend. Maybe things would be returning to normal in a short while? Margaret's train of thought was interrupted by the sound of an approaching vehicle.

"I hope you haven't had breakfast yet because I've brought you something from the kitchen," called out Brian from the driver's seat of his ten-year-old Ford pickup.

Margaret began staring at the truck, her lip turned up to show her displeasure. "I can't believe you drive around in a piece of shit like this," she barked.

"What do you mean—a piece of shit!"

"Brian, haven't you heard the expression 'you are what you drive'?" Margaret asked.

Brian responded by staring silently at Margaret for a few seconds, seemingly collecting his thoughts. "Okay Maggie, if what you say is true, then I guess that stuff that Martin Luther King said about people being judged by the content of their character must be a bunch of crap. I guess you and your yuppie friends have found the real basis for judgment. I'm really impressed Maggie May, really impressed," jested Brian. Margaret glared over the deck railing at Brian, then decided to change the subject.

"I don't plan on paying for another meal the rest of the week. I was just sitting here waiting for you to bring me breakfast," she declared.

"Two blueberry and two bran muffins. Take your pick, Maggie May."

"Bran muffins are for old farts—like you, Brian. I'll take the blueberry, but one should be enough."

Brian ducked inside the cottage and returned with a knife and a tub of margarine. They talked for a few minutes while Margaret had her first food of the day. At one point she got up and refilled both of their cups with some freshly brewed coffee. Soon, Brian picked up on what appeared to be a mood swing from his houseguest.

"Maggie, you're acting a little withdrawn all of a sudden. Are you, by any chance, having some misgivings about that whole thing last night?" Brian appeared concerned.

"Oh God, Brian—no!" She leaned over to him and put her head on his shoulder.

"Last night was fantastic. Now look at me, right in the eyes. It was absolutely fantastic. I just started thinking about this thing back at the office and now my mind's going a hundred miles an hour thinking it all through, that's all."

"Any chance of you letting me in on it?" he asked.

"Any chance of you taking me for a walk down at the beach? I can fill you in on the whole mess while we walk," she said.

Brian agreed, and after letting his guest get fully dressed, he guided her down the street toward the Atlantic. The ocean was about 500 feet away. They ignored the formality of walking to the nearest right-of-way to the beach. Instead, they passed through the yard of an out-of-state property owner whose house sat empty this time of the year. Margaret expressed some concern about trespassing but Brian shrugged it off. Assisting Margaret over an oceanfront barrier, Brian led her down a mound of smooth stones and onto the beach. After reaching the edge of the breaking surf, Margaret began filling Brian in on the details of the Vern and Sara Butler situation. Margaret explained how she was having second thoughts about her decision to dismiss him. Brian listened silently through her entire explanation, saying nothing until she had concluded her account of the events. By now his arm was bent around her tight, slender waist.

"So what have you decided to do about all this?" he asked.

"I'm thinking I might call him Sunday night when I get home," she replied.

"Why would you wait 'til Sunday? You can call him right now and get it over with. Aren't you afraid he might find another job in the meantime?" questioned Brian.

"I don't think there's too much chance of that with the recession and all." It was clear to Brian that Margaret had already considered this possibility.

"Okay, Keogh, forget the chance you might lose him. What about the fact that he's probably worried shitless about his wife, and about not having a job in a couple of weeks? Why not give him a break and take a little of the pressure off of him. What's wrong with calling him now?" Brian spoke accusingly.

"I'm not exactly looking forward to making this call. I'm sure you can understand that. It can wait until Sunday." Margaret barked out her words, showing Brian she did not appreciate being badgered.

"So you plan on carrying this around with you the rest of the week. Why procrastinate? It sounds like you've pretty much made up your mind to ask him back. So, just do it!" Margaret immediately took exception to his admonishing tone.

"You know, I'm sorry I told you anything about this. It's really none of your goddamm business, just get off my ass!" exploded Margaret.

Brian saw that his strategy was not working and decided on a different tact. He stepped in behind her and placed his hands on her shoulders. Moments later, he was rubbing the base of her neck. Margaret sensed immediately that he was extending her an olive branch but she remained silent.

"You're afraid he's going to tell you to go to hell or something, right?" queried Brian.

"It's nothing like that. I just feel stupid about the whole thing. When I did it I wasn't thinking straight. Tax season does that to you."

"Listen, Keogh, if it makes you feel better, I'll share some of my bonehead blunders with you—most of which came during July and August, my busy season. You may find this hard to believe, but even mental giants like myself can screw up once in a while." Margaret managed a weak smile but indicated with a nod that this would not be necessary. They continued to walk beside the crashing sea where they were occasionally forced to jump back from the churning tide.

"Listen, Maggie May, why don't you pack up your things at the lodge this afternoon and move down to the beach with me for the rest of the week? There's no point paying for your room when you can stay with me," offered Brian. Margaret jumped on his offer, accepting it immediately.

"Sounds good to me. I'll pack up this afternoon. One thing though Brian, you don't plan on charging me for last night, do you? I mean, I didn't actually stay at the lodge," she reasoned.

"Maybe you didn't, but your luggage did. I'll have to charge you for the room for both nights Maggie," answered Brian regretfully.

"I don't believe this! You're serious! You're actually going to charge me for two nights," replied Margaret in astonishment. At this point Brian could not tell if she was serious or merely badgering him for the sheer joy of it.

"Jesus, I guess you really are part Scottish. My God—are you cheap!"

"I'll bet if I were prettier, a ten maybe, you wouldn't be charging me for two nights," she said with a straight face.

"Oh please, not that again. Keogh, you're a devastating nine! There probably isn't a more alluring woman within twenty miles of us. You're gorgeous!" trumpeted Brian in frustration.

"Twenty miles?"

"A hundred miles," he insisted. With that concession, Margaret relented as a grin widened across her face. She was looking off into the distance.

"What's that thing way up ahead of us that goes out into the ocean?" She pointed toward a rocky expanse about a mile north.

"That thing is called a jetty. It's at the mouth of Wells Harbor."

"That'd be a great place to run. Maybe you and me could race there some morning before breakfast—loser pays for breakfast." Margaret looked up at Brian for his reaction to her challenge.

"No way, Keogh. It's a no-win situation for me. If I win, big deal, I beat a girl. If I lose, then Maggie May has yet another thing to work me over for. I think I'll pass."

Seconds later, Margaret was making clucking sounds in his ear. "Damn it, Keogh. You come up here with your fancy car and your money. You rub it in our faces. You make sure everyone knows you're smarter than me, you've got more money than me, you're better-looking than me, but that's not enough! Now you want to see if you can prove you're a better athlete than me. That body of yours tells me that you're probably quite the little runner, probably a real thoroughbred. I'm a plodder when it comes to running. I will not let you make me look bad." Margaret saw that Brian was kidding with her. However, she also knew there existed a grain of truth in his words.

Following a twenty-minute stroll, the couple broke away from the shoreline and walked back toward the cottage. Before arriving back at the cottage, Margaret asked Brian if he would hang around a few minutes while she made a phone call. Brian nodded yes.

Margaret walked directly into the house on her arrival back at the property, then sat down on the floor next to the telephone.

"Jesus, Brian—a rotary phone!" she crowed.

"I've got to save money—in anticipation of astronomical accounting and tax consultation fees," he replied. Margaret smiled but the stress associated with her call to the office was already showing on her face. Brian sat on the couch behind her, cradling the back of her head in his hands. She dialed the phone, giving a series disgusted sighs as her finger turned the dial on the outdated telephone.

"Margaret Keogh-Olson and Associates," came the response at the other end of the line.

"Hello, Gretchen, it's Margaret. Anything exciting to report?"

"No, Margaret, everything's under control back here. Are you calling from home?" asked the young secretary.

"No, I'm still in Maine," stated Margaret definitively.

"How's your getaway working out?"

"Well, I'm managing to clear my head up here. Gretchen, is Vern in the office and is he free?"

"Let me check. Hold on, Margaret." After a few moments, Margaret heard a familiar voice on the telephone.

"Vern Butler."

"Hello, Vern, it's Margaret. Do you have a minute?" she asked tentatively.

"Of course, Margaret, I'm glad you called. I needed to speak to you and I wasn't sure how to contact you." Margaret noticed that her senior employee's speech was hurried and ill at ease. "I know you asked me to get my things out of the office by the end of the month,

•

but I was wondering if I could get a short extension. We're having family up from New Jersey and I'd prefer not to...."

"Vern, that's what I'm calling about." Margaret paused briefly as she groped for the proper words and the courage to deliver them.

"I've had some time to think about things at the office—and our meeting last week." She paused, causing an uncomfortable silence. "I was wondering if there was some way for me to convince you to stay with us? And to forget we ever had that meeting last week? There is no excuse for the mistake I made. I think I let the exhaustion from the tax season get to me. I don't know what I was thinking." Brian leaned forward and observed tears welling up in Margaret's eyes.

"You're asking me to stay?" asked Vern.

"I'm asking you to stay, and I'm asking you to forget that I could do anything as stupid as what I did last week. If you've already found another position I'll understand, but I still want to apologize for this unfortunate mess."

"In all honesty, I haven't even begun looking. I haven't even told Sarah yet and I don't even think anyone in the office knows."

"Well, then, maybe we can just keep this between ourselves? I'm not very proud of myself," she confessed.

"You've been out straight for the last four months, young lady. You've been doing your work and half of mine. I think a little slip up once in a while can be expected." Vern was speaking in his wise, fatherly voice as Margaret broke out in a slight smile at her end of the line.

"You sound like you're coming around to being like your old self again with this time off. Any chance Brad has had something to do with this?"

"No, Vern, nothing like that. I'm just spending a little time up in Maine with an old friend. What do you say we grab a little lunch together next week?"

"It's a date," answered Vern. "Margaret, I can't tell you how much pressure this takes off of me. I wasn't looking forward to job hunting out there in the recession, not at my age." Vern's voice began to break up at the end of the sentence. The sound of Vern's emotion had an immediate effect on Margaret as she sat on the living room floor.

"You're the only employee I ever paid with an IOU. That's got to count for something, Vern," stated Margaret. She was making reference to a week four years earlier when she was forced to ask Vern to go without a paycheck for a short period. It was a time when her fledgling firm was experiencing severe cash-flow problems.

"Margaret, if it's okay with you I'd like to wrap this phone call up before I make a complete jackass of myself." Vern's voice quavered.

"Enough said, I'll see you at the office Monday. Say hi to Sarah for me." Margaret hung up the phone and let out a long sigh, her face wet with tears. Brian, who had remained completely silent through the phone conversation, studied his old friend's demeanor as she regained her composure.

"You know, Keogh, as much as I like the cocky wise-ass you are ninety-nine percent of the time, I sort of like this side of you, too." Brian began kissing the top of her head as Margaret remained seated below him on the floor.

"You like me because of my great body, and because I'm so cute and sexy. I'm a nine you know, almost a ten!" Margaret's relief following the Vern Butler call was evident in an observable mood swing.

"Brian, if you're a good boy and don't make me angry the rest of the day, I might let you give me a long, long massage tonight." She sat up, wrapped her arms around him, and rested her head on his chest.

"Now you don't have to spend the rest of your time up here worrying about what's going to happen when you get home. You can thank me now Keogh, say the words. Come on Maggie May, say the words. Say, thank you, Brian." Margaret kept her face buried in his chest for a few seconds before looking up.

"Kelly, I'll be getting a full two-hour massage tonight, not some sixty-minute quickie like that thing last night, right?" Margaret knew she did not have to say the words "thank you." She had said it with the hug and they both knew it.

Moments later, Margaret and Brian stepped outside. They spent a few minutes walking around the edge of the property, looking out over the estuary. They quietly watched as a formation of geese flew above them heading due north. The tide was silently filling in the muddy coves of the estuary. Brian asked Margaret if she would like to go on a canoe ride before she left for home, and she responded with an enthusiastic yes. Soon they were driving up Mile Road to the lodge.

That afternoon Margaret packed her luggage, settled her bill, and moved everything down to the beach cottage.

11

B RIAN WAS STILL ASLEEP WHEN Margaret opened her eyes on Sunday morning. On awakening, the first thought to run through her mind was that she would be leaving Maine later in the day. Margaret was amazed how the last five days with Brian had flown by. She recalled the events of the week as she rested between the bedcovers. She thought of the emotional surge that swept over her when she awakened to the sight of Brian in the TV room at the lodge. There was Brian's clumsy effort as he brought coffee to her in the fifties room on the first morning, followed by their return to Parson's Beach after nearly two decades. Margaret thought back to her massage at the cottage and the lovemaking that followed that night, and every night since. The bicycle rides to Ogunquit and Kennebunkport, the five-mile jogs along Moody and Crescent beaches; these events added up and had made for a wonderful getaway. She had resolved the problem with Vern Butler, after some prodding from Brian, and even paddled the canoe to dinner with Brian one evening, returning just ahead of the retreating tidewater.

Margaret thought of her time in Maine over the last five days as the kind of experiences written about in dreadful romance novels. These were the sort of books she had avoided for the better part of her thirty-four years. The thought of leaving this place saddened her. She considered the past five days and realized that they may have been the best five days of her life. Margaret asked herself, was that really possible?

She had always known that the happiest day of her life was the day Jenny was born, but that was just one day. The second happiest day of her life? That had to be the day she received notification she had passed the CPA exam. The third happiest was her wedding day. These were all wonderful days but they were single days. Margaret was rapidly coming to the conclusion that she had never been as happy as this—her five days with Brian Kelly on the coast of Maine.

Five days earlier, she had left a successful, albeit stressful, tax season behind her and traveled to the Maine coast. Her mission to rectify a dreadful mistake from her youth had resulted in the awakening of passion and an end to a prolonged period of celibacy. Margaret was becoming depressed. Brian rolled over. He was facing her now. As if sensing she was awake, he opened his eyes.

"What are you thinking about?" he asked, still only partly awake.

"About having to go home—having to leave all of this pampering behind," Margaret answered.

"Can't you find anyone to pamper you back in Manchester?"

"Oh, I guess I could, but they wouldn't be as good at it as you. You have a real gift for it, Kelly." She chuckled and patted him on the cheek. They both knew that their relationship was partly adversarial. However, this did nothing to diminish what they felt toward one another. They were both bright and they loved matching wits.

"Oh, I see—so when God was handing out talents to everyone, he passed on things like good looks, high intellect and super strength for me and just made me good at pampering Maggie May Keogh. Is that it?" asked Brian, feigning scorn.

Margaret smiled at him at close range and nodded yes. "Oh Brian, here's something else to think about. Every relationship like ours needs to have a dominant partner and a submissive partner. Now, why don't you get out of bed and squeeze me some orange juice before you make us coffee. Meantime, while you're doing that, see if you can figure out your role in this relationship all by yourself," said Margaret patronizingly.

The words had hardly passed her lips when Brian lurched across the bed and pulled her naked body against his, covering her mouth with his own. They held the embrace for the better part of a minute, never letting their eager tongues disengage. Brian was running his hands over the well-defined curves of her body. Margaret felt his tongue on her neck sucking on her skin uncontrollably. He rolled their bodies over, reversing positions and bringing her body atop his. He pulled her closer and she felt his organ against her. It was already hard and erect. Margaret knew she wanted him inside her. She grabbed hold of his penis and directed it deep within her. They were so familiar with one another by now that every movement seem perfectly orchestrated. Her head tossed back in reflex as he drove inside her. Over and over he pushed himself deeper and deeper within her physical being...making them one...making them one...making them one. Brian sucked upon her perfumed skin as his mouth ran over her face, neck and arms. She cried out. Margaret was already there where pleasure is almost too great to bear, where pleasure almost becomes a threat to physical well-being.

"Have you reached orgasm yet?" he asked in a whisper.

"You don't have to wait for me this time, Brian. Go ahead, it's all right." With that Brian rolled them over again. His mouth returned to her neck...drawing...sucking...biting. His animal instincts were dictating their actions. Rational thought was ruled out. This further excited her. Margaret began her euphoric explosion just as he cried out. The liquefied passion harnessed within them was being released as they both struggled for additional seconds of passionate bliss. They were drowning in each other. Time passed but it was immeasurable. Brian was first to slowly initiate the separation of their bodies. Margaret breathed deeply as her sex organs granted her a few additional moments of uncompromising pleasure. Upon separation, Brian leaned down and licked the beads of perspiration from between her breasts. She smiled and kissed him again on the mouth. Moments later, they were lying beside each other.

It was Margaret's voice that interrupted the quiet in the room.

"Brian, I think I'm in love with you." Her words appeared to come involuntarily. At this moment she had no power over what she said or did. She needed him too much to have any measure of power.

"I remember the exact moment I fell in love with you, the exact moment." Brian was not leaving Margaret to dangle alone with her admission.

"And when was that?" she asked.

"I walked into a strange classroom, in a new school, and was assigned my homeroom desk. As I approached the desk, I saw the most beautiful girl I had ever laid eyes on begin removing her things from the desk. She glared at me and my stomach knotted up. I was in trouble and I knew it." Brian was looking deep into her eyes as he spoke.

"Oh my God, you remember that! I can't believe you still remember that!" exclaimed Margaret.

"How could I forget the first time I laid eyes on you?" asked Brian. She reached out to him, and then pulled his body against hers. As Margaret held him, she thought how wonderful it was to communicate with another human being on this level. They were being completely honest and speaking without inhibition.

"You asked me earlier what I was thinking about. I was just kidding with that nonsense about pampering and all." As she spoke, Margaret revealed an honesty that was not evident only days earlier.

"I was thinking about my life before I came up here and found you. Here I was with a husband who was living with another woman—and with no end in sight on that front—not to mention a daughter who'll be moving out of the house in September and living in Rhode Island nine months a year. I was probably going to be all alone in the next few months and the thought of it was scaring the shit out of me. The way it had just snuck up on me. I was going to be alone. But, now this—you—us."

"You get used to it, Maggie. It's not the hell you seem to be building in your imagination."

"Are you saying I'm going to be alone anyway—no Brian Kelly?"

"Come on, Keogh, you know I'm yours for the asking. I'm just saying that being alone is not as bad as you're making it out to be. I speak of this from experience. May I ask you something deeply personal?" Brian was perfectly serious at this point in the discussion.

"Sure, go ahead," Margaret answered guardedly.

"You talk about your husband living with another woman with no end in sight. Well, I guess I'd like to know what happens if he comes crawling back."

"I don't see that happening," responded Margaret instantly.

"I didn't ask you if you saw that happening. I asked you what happens if he does come back." Margaret saw Brian focused intently on her, specifically her eyes. He seemed to be looking for any intonation in her voice or unguarded mannerism. Brian was looking for an unspoken message.

"To be totally honest, up until five days ago I would have taken him back. I had expected him back by now, but more and more it's beginning to look like he's found what he wants in his young friend. That was a lot harder to deal with before I found you. I know I couldn't give you up at this point. I trust you Brian, and you have to learn to trust me." He stared into Margaret's face, smiled faintly, but said nothing.

Over the next few hours Margaret's luggage was packed and she and Brian managed to squeeze in a final stroll at the edge of the Atlantic. With her BMW loaded for the journey home, they drove back up to the lodge. Margaret wanted to say good-bye to Millie. But first, she slipped away to revisit the fifties room. It seemed a long time since she took refuge there. Five days earlier she stepped inside this room with Brian Kelly nothing more than a hazy figure from her past. She took a last glance at the pictures of Ike and Marilyn and closed the door behind her. She came downstairs just as Brian and Millie were wrapping up a discussion about a Memorial Day weekend package.

Millie shot a subtle wink at Margaret, out of Brian's view, and asked if she could speak to her. The two women strolled into the TV room and Millie ushered Margaret to a far corner.

"Young lady, I know it's none of my business, but I'm not one to leave my two cents out of anything. He's been real private when it's come to anything about the two of you. Put an old woman's mind to rest and tell me you two are planning to go on seeing each other." Millie was resting her hand on Margaret's arm and speaking just above a whisper.

"Millie, you don't have much to worry about along those lines," answered Margaret.

"Because, I'll tell you—they don't come much better than that one in the next room. I just hope you know what you have there." Margaret gave Millie a nod before kissing her softly on the cheek. Then, the two women returned to Brian's side at the front desk.

As Margaret's departure drew closer, Brian's mood became increasingly solemn. He walked her to the BMW, not uttering a word. Reaching the car, she whirled around and confronted him.

"Are you going to let me bring my daughter up with me next weekend? Or will that cramp your style?" Margaret knew she had to lighten things before proceeding any further down the driveway.

"I don't care if you bring Ringling Brothers, Barnum and Bailey with you, just come." Margaret's question seemed to relieve some of Brian's anxiety.

"You'll be relegated to the couch," she warned with a smile. Brian responded with a resigned sigh and wrapped his arms around her. There was a final, prolonged meeting of their lips before Margaret turned away and climbed inside her car. She touched his hand through the window before pulling out of the parking lot and rolling up the driveway to Route 1. In her side-view mirror, Margaret saw that he did not look away until sometime after she turned south into the Route 1 traffic.

12

For the next month and a half Margaret spent each weekend on the Maine coast at Wells Beach. On most of these weekends she was accompanied by Jenny, who quickly developed a fondness for Brian. On those weekends when Jenny was along, Brian and Margaret would manage to arrange personal time by wandering off to an isolated, unoccupied cottage in the complex. Brian would privately run down a list of vacant units and Margaret would select a cottage or motel room she had not seen. An hour later the two would suddenly reappear on the complex grounds. A short, subdued phone call from Molly announcing her intention to remain in Vermont after final exams effectively ended her relationship with Brian, much to his relief.

Jenny was scheduled to graduate on June 8. This would mark the first weekend since the close of tax season that her mother would stay home in New Hampshire and not visit Brian in Maine. On the Sunday prior to her graduation, Jenny and her mother returned home to Bedford in the early evening. That evening, after unpacking and throwing together a makeshift dinner, Margaret answered the phone in her home office.

"Hello, Margaret, it's Brad. I wonder if you have a minute?" The call caught Margaret off guard.

"Yes, I guess I do. Is anything wrong?" she asked.

"No, nothing like that. I was calling to see if we could arrange to meet somewhere next week and talk over some matters?" Brad was being vague.

"Could you give me an inkling of what you have on your mind, Brad?" she asked, sounding mildly put out.

"Margaret, I've contacted a lawyer down here and asked him to assist me in filing for divorce. I've asked Becky to marry me and she's accepted." Margaret felt a terrible pressure growing in her stomach at the news.

"Perhaps we could grab lunch next week and discuss things calmly?" he injected.

"What day is good for you?" she asked emotionlessly.

"I'm flexible, whatever works for you. I'll come up to New Hampshire," offered Brad.

"If it's all right with you, I'd like to do this away from Manchester," Margaret replied, her mind still reeling from the shock of the news.

"What about that Mexican place in Merrimack we used to go to on the way home from Patriot games?" asked Brad.

"That'll be fine. How about Tuesday at noon?" she suggested.

Brad accepted, and without any further conversation or meaningless chitchat the telephone call was mercifully brought to a close. Margaret robotically rose from behind her desk and walked across the hall to Jenny's room. After applying three raps, and being cleared to enter, Margaret stood in the doorway until Jenny lifted her eyes from a text book.

"That was your stepfather on the phone. He said he wants a divorce." Margaret spoke the words as if only to provide the information to her daughter as a courtesy. She intentionally left her emotions out of her speech.

Over the next thirty-six hours, Margaret prepared for the luncheon meeting with her husband. She updated their personal financial statement and calculated their combined net worth. Margaret became concerned about the potential or estimated value of her accounting practice. The value of her office building was pretty much washed out by the existing mortgage on the property, but the potential market value of her client base was substantial. Margaret juggled these issues in her head while she reminded herself to treat the luncheon as a business meeting and not as a personal confrontation. Margaret was aware of her aversion to personal confrontations. She theorized that her success at this meeting would probably depend upon how well she managed to keep the discussion focused on business.

Margaret arrived at the restaurant first and requested a booth within sight of the front door. With no sign of Brad at the moment, she began rearranging the table top in such a way that all of the ornaments, condiment bottles, and the like were cluttered largely on the side away from her. Years before, she had read somewhere that crowded table tops sometime had an unsettling effect, even if subconscious, on an unwary victim. She reasoned that if it meant even the slightest advantage for her, then it was worth the effort. Margaret simply did not know what to expect. In the past, Margaret had usually managed to get her way on matters when Brad and her were at odds. Considering that Brad already had spoken to a lawyer, she had no idea what to expect. What she did know was that if Brad decided to get greedy she would remind him of the circumstances behind the divorce. She would underscore who had earned the lion's share of their assets, and hint at exactly how uncomfortable she was willing to make it for him, if prodded. Margaret knew he was a proud man, and the prospect of this kind of public procedure was, no doubt, unpleasant for him. Margaret was gearing herself up for the worst.

She glanced down at her watch as Brad appeared in the doorway— eleven fifty-eight, not bad, she thought. Margaret signaled to him as his eyes scanned the dining area. Seconds later, they were sharing their first eye-to eye contact in five months. Brad seemed unnaturally relaxed as he inquired about Margaret's, and then Jenny's, well being. This was followed by the obligatory inquiries into the financial health of her accounting practice. Margaret grew uneasy with the formality of the discussion. As lunch was ordered, and the conversation began to falter, she decided to steer the discussion toward business.

"I've taken the liberty of preparing a rough, combined personal financial statement. I thought we could begin there, maybe reach a preliminary agreement on—"

"Margaret, before you go any further, I'd like to just toss something out. It's not like I'm some innocent party here. We're here today because of my actions, not yours. I'll make this very simple. If I can walk away with ten-thousand dollars in cash and my car, I'll sign off on everything else." Margaret began running the math in her head as Brad continued to speak. She estimated that Brad was offering to settle for less than three percent of their net worth, and that did not even factor in the market value of her practice.

She stared emotionlessly into his eyes, displaying no positive or negative reaction.

"I realize it was mostly your money that paid for the house and the cottage in North Conway. The ten-thousand dollars is just to get me started again." Amazingly, he was practically apologizing for what was more than a reasonable request. Margaret noted that Brad was not mentioning Becky.

"And you'll assume total responsibility for the outstanding balance on your car loan?" Margaret asked, already beginning to carve the settlement conditions in stone. Brad nodded in agreement.

Moments later, their waitress was placing their meals in front of them and for a few minutes the conversation reverted back to light banter. Margaret got the impression Brad was growing more tense as the luncheon progressed. She felt herself begin to relax as the tightness in her stomach eased. She had come, expecting a confrontation on some level, and now it appeared she was presiding over an unconditional surrender.

"Margaret, do you think there might be some way we could work out something so my folks could use the mountain cottage once in a while?" asked Brad, almost as an afterthought. Brad referred to a cottage in the White Mountains that was a year-round rental property. They had purchased this small house eight years earlier. The story behind how it had been acquired had become family lore.

As the story went, Margaret had learned of the availability of this small house in the middle of New Hampshire's White Mountains from a client. The owner, a widower, was presumably at wits' end searching for a buyer. No one would agree to his price and he had been insulted by most of the offers he had received. Supposedly, Margaret drove to North Conway on a Saturday in October and offered the man a rock-bottom price, but threw in a ten-year-old recreational vehicle she had picked up from a destitute client. Margaret's offer was no better than any other offer this man had fielded to date. However, she had just thrown this tiny wrinkle, a secondhand recreational vehicle, into the deal. In her mind, she provided him not only with the money to leave, but also something to leave in. The deal was closed less than a week later. The purchase of their mountain cottage provided Brad Olson with the first inkling of his new wife's resourcefulness. Over the years, the cottage evolved into a rental property.

"Why don't you take it? Your mom and dad have always watched over it for us. I think it's only fair it stays in your family. If everything else goes down as agreed, I think I can live with this settlement," said Margaret. Brad appeared genuinely astonished by Margaret's display of generosity.

In the remaining time, Brad explained to Margaret that his attorney would wait until contacted by someone representing her. It was his hope that the entire process could be streamlined, perhaps resulting in finalization by the end of the year. The luncheon concluded with a handshake and a mutual promise of cooperation. Sitting behind the wheel of her car in the parking lot, Margaret watched as the man with whom she had shared the last nine years, fastened his seat belt, adjusted his rearview mirror, and drove out of her life. She was overcome by exactly how little effort it seemed to take. It had been re-fined, almost clinical. Margaret thought of Brian for a moment, then started her car and drove north back to Manchester.

Arriving back at her office, Margaret phoned Claire and asked if she could join her for a drink after work. They arranged to meet in the lounge of the Marketplace Restaurant, just off the highway exit in Bedford. Next came a call to the house to leave a message for Jenny that she would not be arriving home until seven or seven thirty. A few hours later, Margaret entered the lounge ahead of Claire and took a corner table at the rear of the room. Claire strode through the door just as Margaret was placing her order. The two friends exchanged pleas-antries while waiting on their beverages. Margaret was first to change the mood of the conversation as she broke the news to her friend.

"Brad has asked me for a divorce," stated Margaret. Claire's eyes widened.

"When?"

"Officially, at lunch today. He actually called me on Sunday night and broke the news. He has asked his young friend to marry him and, presumably, she has accepted."

"Are you okay?" asked Claire. She appeared concerned.

"To be honest, it's bothering me a little more than I would have expected, considering how well things are going with Brian and all," admitted Margaret.

"So, if he told you about his plans Sunday night, why the meeting today?"

"Today we began discussing the financial arrangements. As a mat-ter of fact, we began and ended the discussion today. He's pretty much conceding most of the property to me. He wants to streamline the pro-cess and keep the lawyer's time at a minimum. It makes sense."

"He probably wants to avoid turning this into a pissing contest. Are you completely satisfied with your share?" Claire asked.

"Yes, without question," answered Margaret with no hesitation. A smile broke across Margaret's face as she thought back on her lun-cheon meeting earlier that day. Claire noticed the look on her face.

"What's so amusing?" asked Claire.

"I wouldn't admit this to anyone but you," said Margaret with a sheepish grin, "I got to the restaurant before Brad and decided to use that crazy thing where I push everything on the table to the other side, you know, to get the other person uptight and flustered." Claire knew immediately what Margaret was talking about, having once served as a guinea pig for her friend. They both broke out in spontaneous laughter.

"Well, that explains why Brad conceded everything so easily," exclaimed Claire. There was more laughter followed by an extended period of silence as the two women sipped on their beverages. "So, when do I get a chance to meet the new man in your life?"

"He's coming down this Friday night for Jenny's graduation. He'll be at the house for a while but I think he'll have to go back to Maine that night. Come to think of it, I'm not so sure I want him getting a look at you, friend or no friend."

Claire laughed at the compliment. "And how is Jenny reacting to her mother's new romantic interest?"

"Oh God, Jenny loves Brian. The two are always clowning around when they're together. Oh, before I forget, do you know anyone I can call—a lawyer I mean—to represent me in this thing with Brad? I know a couple dozen lawyers but not one divorce attorney."

"Yes!" Claire's voice rose in response to Margaret's question. "I knew there was something else I wanted to tell you about. Last weekend I attended an open house at Eggleston, Sanders & Cohen and they were introducing a new partner they had just brought over from Portsmouth, Attorney Reid Birmingham. Margaret, he is absolutely gorgeous. Oh, and listen to this. His family is the fourth richest in New Hampshire. I'm not through. Last year he was voted one of the ten most-eligible bachelors in New England! Not New Hampshire—New England. Old man Eggleston says with this guy's money, charm, good looks and brains, he can see him running for governor in another five to ten years." Margaret could see that this new attorney had made quite an impression on her friend.

"And how, pray tell, did you find out that his family was the fourth richest in New Hampshire?" asked Margaret bewilderedly.

"Old man Eggleston. He makes it his business to know things like that. Anyway, Reid is a divorce lawyer and supposedly a pretty good one," added Claire.

"Well, it's not like this is going to be a great challenge. It's a no-brainer. Brad and I are in full agreement and I'm going to provide our personal financial statements to both sides."

"Margaret, I'm just saying that this fellow comes highly recommended and you're going to flip when you see what he looks like. One thing though, if you do decide to contact him, be sure to let him know that you were referred by me." Margaret chuckled as she removed a pen from her handbag.

"Claire, you sound just like a teenager. Okay, what's his name again?"

"Reid Birmingham with Eggleston, Sanders & Cohen," answered Claire deliberately.

"I'll call him in the morning," said Margaret.

13

Jenny's graduation ceremony took place in the local civic auditorium on the first Friday in June. This weekend broke the consecutive string of weekends in which Margaret traveled to Maine to be with Brian. Instead, Brian accepted the invitation to join Margaret and her parents at the ceremony. A small gathering of family and friends awaited Jenny back at the house in Bedford after graduation. It was there that Margaret presented her daughter with a 1988 Nissan Sentra, a low-mileage cream puff with air conditioning and carpeted floors. Margaret still remembered how Brian had been slighted at a similar family gathering immediately after Jenny's birth, so she took special care to introduce Brian to her circle of friends, among them Claire.

At one point during the gathering Margaret returned to the living room only to find Claire sitting on Brian's lap, her arm wrapped around his shoulder. Somehow Brian had persuaded Claire to play along with one of his gags. Immediately recognizing a Brian Kelly prank, Margaret decided to give him a little of his own medicine.

"Careful, Claire, that's my butt boy you're flirting with," said Margaret disdainfully. Brian's mouth dropped open and an embarrassed look crossed his face.

"Who are you calling your butt boy?" he asked, sounding very insulted.

"Oh, come on, Brian, let's be honest for God's sake. We always do what I say—when I say it. I never have to pay for anything, that's your job. I get a massage whenever I want, and my foot rubs are on demand. I think that makes you my butt boy." Brian was temporarily at a loss for words.

"Brian, you have to be a little more assertive with this one," said Mrs. Keogh, offering him some motherly advice.

"Mrs. Keogh, she is so full of crap. It's not like that at all," exclaimed Brian in defense of himself.

"Oh Margaret, where can I get one of these?" cried out Claire, holding Brian at arm's length. He could only stare across the room and call out a good-natured threat.

"I'll get you for this," he declared. Margaret glanced back wearing a smug look of satisfaction. She did not speak. She simply moved her lips in such a way that Brian could read them.

"Don't mess with me," was the message he was able to decode.

Prior to breaking away from the gathering of adult well-wishers, Jenny pulled her mother aside for some words in private.

"Mother, I'd like to run something by you before I commit to anything." Margaret gestured to her daughter to continue.

"Trudy Abrams and I have been playing with the idea of working at the beach this summer and I'd like to make sure that it was okay with you. We were thinking of going up to Wells or Ogunquit." She looked into her mother's eyes, searching for a hint to her reaction.

"Isn't it a little late to be just planning this now? Do you think you can find a place to stay at this late date?" Margaret was caught off guard by Jenny's tentative plans. She envisioned a final summer with Jenny at home in Bedford prior to her daughter's departure for Brown.

"Ordinarily, yes, but with Brian helping us we should be able to find something. Now as far as a job or jobs, he says there are always positions opening up all summer. They won't be great jobs but it'll allow us to stash a little something away for September."

"You've discussed this with Brian?" quizzed Margaret.

"Yes, Mother, I didn't want to just jump into this with my eyes closed," responded Jenny.

"And Trudy's parents are ready to go along with something like this?"

"They said that as long as it was someplace respectable like Kennebunkport or Wells, it was all right with them," answered Jenny.

"Well, Jen, give me a night to sleep on it." Margaret decided to stall for time.

"Mother, keep in mind—it's not like I'll be alone up there. I can always run to Brian for help if I screw up." Margaret forced a faint smile but did not reply. After properly thanking everyone for her gifts, Jenny tactfully excused herself from her elders and made haste to join her friends at a party at another house. She departed giddily, anticipating her classmates reaction to her new, secondhand car. Margaret did not waste a moment locating Brian following her daughter's exit.

"So, how long have you known that Jenny was thinking of working up at the beach this summer?" There was an angry tone in Margaret's voice, immediately putting Brian on the defensive.

"Hold it, Maggie, she never came right out and told me she was coming over. She just asked me a few questions a couple of weeks ago." Margaret was making no attempt to hide her displeasure.

"To hear her talk, it sounds like you were a real fount of information. I really don't appreciate you two discussing something like this behind my back."

"Maggie, say the word and I'll completely step back from this whole thing. To be honest, I was a little flattered when Jenny came to me for advice. I probably should've said something to you," admitted Brian.

"She played you like a flute. You don't know teenage girls like I do. I'll just see how this plays out. In the future, think before you open your mouth." With that, Margaret forced a smile and rejoined the crowd in the living room. Brian watched her leave in silence, as a child might following a chastisement from a parent. He paused for a few moments, collected his feelings, then rejoined the gathering in the next room.

Over the next forty-five minutes the crowd of guests shrunk by ones and twos until only Brian, Margaret, and her parents were left to pick up. Mrs. Keogh repeatedly remarked how wonderful it was to see the two old friends together. Finally, Brian asked the Keoghs if they would excuse him and their daughter for just a few moments. With the Keogh's permission, Brian took Margaret's hand and pulled her to the kitchen with Margaret giving playful, mock resistance. Once out of her parent's sight, Brian pushed Margaret against the refrigerator. Then, he leaned his body against hers, held her head between his hands, and showered a series of methodical kisses to her face and mouth. Before withdrawing from against her, Brian inhaled the fragrance from her hair. At last he pulled back.

"That's for treating me like a ten-year-old earlier this evening." He paused and searched her face for a reaction. Predictably, Margaret responded with the same confident smile, the one he had labeled as cocky.

"Oh, one more thing, Keogh—don't ever change." Brian leaned forward and gave her a final, respectable kiss before offering her parents an invitation to visit him in Wells. Margaret walked Brian to the door, thanking him for coming over. They agreed to see each other the following weekend in Maine.

* * *

On Tuesday morning Margaret arrived at the offices of Eggleston, Sanders & Cohen at a few minutes before ten o'clock for an initial meeting.

She had called the law firm the prior week, and on the recommendation of her friend, scheduled a meeting with Attorney Birmingham. The receptionist at the front desk advised her that he would be with her momentarily and directed her to a group of large, leather upholstered chairs in the lobby. From there, Margaret was able to observe the administrative workings of the office. She was also able to monitor the passage of time on the wall clock behind the receptionist's desk. Margaret was experiencing some anxiety with the whole process associated with the ending of her marriage. She gazed intermittently at the clock as the minute hand swept past twelve and downward until finally, at seventeen minutes past the hour, a man descended the stairs and made his way toward her, his hand extended.

"Hello, Mrs. Olson, I'm Reid Birmingham. Why don't you join me up in my office?"

Margaret rose from her chair while looking over the lawyer with curious interest. Although agitated by being kept waiting beyond ten o'clock, she withheld comment. Reid Birmingham was a reasonably fit man in his mid- to late-thirties. He stood about six feet tall, with thick, salt-and-pepper shaded hair that framed a handsome face. He smiled at Margaret while directing her to his office. She thought his smile reflected classic, Anglo-Saxon lineage. After guiding her to the primary visitor's chair in his office, he closed the door and settled back behind his desk. He had a relaxed manner about him as his eyes passed over some notes on his desk.

"I was referred to you by Claire Gagnon from the Chamber of Commerce," offered Margaret as the attorney continued to study his notes.

"Pretty girl," he said distractedly. He raised his eyes to her while making the comment.

"Borderline beautiful is probably more like it," shot back Margaret.

"Are you two close friends?" His attention was now completely focused on Margaret.

"Yes, I think you could say that. We share quite a bit—personally and professionally." Having said that, Margaret decided to get the meeting back on track. She pulled a manila envelope from her briefcase and placed it in front of the lawyer.

"Inside the envelope you will find what I believe will be all of the financial data you will need to assist me in finalizing the divorce. I'm not sure how much background you may have gotten from my phone call last week. I believe I spoke to your assistant or a paralegal aide. In any event, my husband and I have already hashed out the financial conditions of the divorce. We are in complete agreement." The attorney had already begun reviewing the documents taken from inside the envelope. Margaret studied his handsome features while his attention was focused on the paperwork.

"I'm not accustomed to getting information in such a complete and orderly manner," admitted the attorney.

"You'll find a copy of the other attorney's business card in the package. I believe my husband will have spoken to him by now about the conditions and details we have come up with. Mr. Birmingham, I see this whole process as being very cut and dry at your end, and I expect this will be reflected in your billable hours." Margaret spoke authoritatively. Any anxiety she had brought to the meeting was no longer evident.

"You haven't mentioned anything about children and visitation rights. How does that stand?" inquired the attorney.

"I have a daughter, practically eighteen. She, however, is not my husband's biological daughter. I had her prior to our marriage. If she wants to see her stepfather at any time, then that is her affair—no problems on that front. Also, there is nothing in the way of spousal support to be concerned with. What we're trying to do here is keep personal and family matters out of the proceedings. No finger pointing—everything strictly financial," stated Margaret. The lawyer listened while continuing to analyze the financial information in front of him. She saw his eyes stop and focus on something specific.

"Humor me for a moment, Mrs. Olson. My notes state that your husband walked out on you last January and that he has requested the divorce in order to remarry. Would it be safe to assume on my part that it was his infidelity that led to the deterioration of your marriage? I only raise the question in light of the fact that it may be possible for you to retain ownership of the house in North Conway with a slight amount of arm twisting." Margaret stared silently at the lawyer for a few seconds. When she spoke her voice was calm but resolved.

"Counselor, have I been talking for the last five minutes just to hear myself speak?" Their eyes locked as the attorney appeared startled by the woman's rhetorical question. The first syllable of an explanation had just left his mouth when Margaret spoke over him.

"All I need to know at this time is whether you want the engagement or not. If you don't, then simply say so and I will go elsewhere." Margaret's feistiness was more the result of being kept waiting in the lobby earlier than anything Reid Birmingham had said. Inexplicably, there was a bewildered smile on the his face.

"I'll call your husband's attorney this afternoon and confirm that everything at his end agrees with your notes, then I'll report back to you."

Margaret thought the lawyer seemed flustered by the earlier exchange and so mercifully took steps to moderate the tone of the conversation. She reached into her handbag and withdrew a checkbook. "You'll want a retainer for this work. How much, and to whom?"

The lawyer jumped up from his chair and came around the desk. "Why don't we wait until I've had the opportunity to speak to your husband's representative. I will need one of your business cards and perhaps your home phone number," he said. Margaret produced the card and scrawled her home number on the back. Interestingly, she thought she caught the lawyer admiring her crossed legs as she fumbled with her briefcase.

"Your office is just a couple of streets away from here, if I'm not mistaken," he added.

"Yes it is. That must explain why I managed to be on time for our meeting this morning." Her sarcasm was not lost on him as he gave a slight shrug. With that said, she extended her hand.

"It was good meeting you and I look forward to hearing from you. I'll find my own way out." Margaret turned and started down the hallway but not until she gave the handsome attorney a beguiling smile. On the short walk back to the office Margaret cautioned herself to be careful. The lawyer had made an impact on her in spite of their short time together.

The phone rang in Margaret's office late in the afternoon that same day. It was Claire. Seconds after lifting the receiver, Margaret knew her friend had something of particular interest to report.

"What went on at your meeting with Reid Birmingham this morning? I just got off the phone with him and I'm not sure what to make of the conversation," blurted out Claire.

"What do you mean?" Margaret responded. She was being coy with her friend, knowing Claire must have gotten feedback about the meeting, but decided to downplay the matter, at least on the surface.

"What do I mean? What do I mean? Reid calls, presumably to thank me for the referral, and the next thing I know he's asking me all these personal questions about you."

"Like what kind of questions?" Margaret was no longer trying to conceal her interest.

"Oh, like were you heavily involved with anyone at present and did we socialize together. He went so far as to ask me if I thought you were up to meeting new people and developing new relationships. God, Margaret, what did you do to pique his interest like this?" Margaret was laughing as she took in her friend's astonished reaction.

"Claire, I was an absolute bitch. For starters, he kept me waiting in the lobby for over fifteen minutes without so much as an explanation or apology, and that sort of set me off. He must have been expecting the poor, shattered woman routine from me and I caught him off guard. By the way, what did you tell him, about me I mean? Did you say anything about Brian?"

"No, I played dumb. I think I said you were slowly getting yourself back on track and—oh, he asked me if you were a man-hater!" Margaret exploded with laughter at his question.

"God, I must have been even more of a bitch than I thought. Are you sure you're not reading your conversation with him all wrong? Claire, why on earth would he be interested, given what I told you?" she asked.

"The guy is probably accustomed to having women gushing all over him, and then along comes the CPA from hell and then he's not sure what hit him. I swear, if you weren't my closest friend, I'd hate you. Margaret, you have to admit, the man is gorgeous," exclaimed Claire.

"He is quite good looking," admitted Margaret. She always avoided the use of feminine adjectives when describing attractive males.

"So, did he drop any hints about what his plans were?" questioned Margaret coyly.

"No, not really, but take my word for it—the guy is interested— very, very interested. I'll wager you a lunch that he makes a move inside of a week." Margaret responded with more laughter.

"This is so strange, Claire. Tell me, what do I do if he gets back to me and shows interest? Do I ruin my image and show him my better side, or do I continue busting his balls?" Claire let out a howl, causing her friend to pull the phone from her ear.

"That's something you'll have to decide on your own my friend. In the meantime, just remember—the fourth richest family in the state— the fourth-richest family in the state—the fourth—"

"I get the message, Claire," interrupted Margaret. She asked her friend to keep her advised of any additional news from this front and brought the conversation to a close as she rolled back in her chair, mulling over this development. It was pleasant to hear that she had made an impression on Reid Birmingham. However, Margaret was already developing conflicting emotions from these developments involving Mr. Birmingham. She pondered how this might impact her relationship with Brian, then laughed at herself for jumping to such a silly conclusion. She reasoned that Reid Birmingham will likely have forgotten who she was by dinner.

Margaret put in another ninety minutes at the office before driving home to Bedford. Her mood dampened after she arrived, finding Jenny in the midst of packing for her summer move to Maine. Jenny and Trudy Abrams would set out the following day for southern Maine. They were scheduled to meet with a Mrs. Littlefield in Ogunquit to arrange for summer accommodations. If things did not work out with Mrs. Littlefield, Brian would provide them with lodging, at least temporarily. She summoned up a reserve of strength to mask her disappointment. The thought that she would not have her daughter around the house this final summer before college depressed her. It was clear to her how much this adventure meant to Jenny, and for that reason she masked her true emotions. Margaret was already experiencing a preview of the loneliness that she could expect in only twenty-four hours. Tomorrow night, she would be all alone in her expansive, white colonial.

Margaret shrugged off the pensive mood that began to cast a shroud over her and suggested that the two Keogh women make a night of it. Jenny gladly opted to finish her packing the next morning and joined her mother for dinner at the Marketplace Restaurant, less than a mile from the house. During the evening the observant teenager thought she detected a touch of sadness in her mother. Jenny quickly reminded her how wonderful it would be seeing her every weekend during her visits with Brian. They kidded back and forth about how Jenny the waitress could be confronted by her mother at any time throughout the summer. However, behind all the good-humored kidding, they both knew they were saying good-bye; not a total good-bye or a final good-bye, but some manner of good-bye. Their lives were reaching a crossroads and they both knew it.

After seeing Jenny off, Margaret arrived at her office just before eight o'clock the next morning. She barely had time to organize her desk and pour a cup of coffee when Gretchen announced that she had a call from Attorney Birmingham .

"Good morning, Mr. Birmingham, what's up?" Margaret spoke in her typical pleasant, no-nonsense manner.

"Well, Mrs. Olson, it does appear that your take on the matter of the distribution of assets with your husband was pretty much on the money. I spoke to his attorney late yesterday and it appears that he is planning to proceed with the process according to details as indicated by you. I have forwarded a copy of your financial information to his office in Boston and he will report on it to your husband. Once we get an okay from them we can put things in motion."

"I'm glad to hear it."

"Listen, Margaret, I was wondering if we could get together, maybe over lunch, and go over something involving the divorce that concerns me?"

"Anything real important?" asked Margaret, the slightest trace of concern creeping into her voice.

"No, nothing like that. Just something at my end," added the lawyer.

"Well, lunch is definitely out today, but tomorrow might work. How's Thursday with you?" she asked.

"I'll make it work. Are you partial to anyplace in particular? You're the local."

"Let me give it some thought. You're not that far away. Why don't you drop by at about 11:45 tomorrow morning and I'll give you the twenty-five-cent tour." Reid agreed and the appointment was finalized. Margaret immersed herself back into her work but could not help wondering what the handsome attorney had to discuss that required a face-to-face meeting.

Margaret finished up one of her customary ten-hour days at 6:45 on Wednesday evening. After clearing her desk and signing off her computer she walked through the quiet office building and out to the car. As she cruised the downtown streets and crossed the Merrimack River, she realized this day would be like no other in memory. There would be no daughter or husband to greet, or be greeted by, when she arrived at the house in Bedford. There would not be the comfort of a parent's smile or hug to welcome her home. For the first time in Margaret Keogh-Olson's life, she was a single individual in the truest sense. Approaching the house on its U-shaped driveway, it looked bigger than before. It seemed ready to swallow her as she entered the front door.

Upon entering, the first thing she noticed was the total absence of sound. She grabbed the TV remote on her way through the living room and clicked on the television. Channel-surfing for only a few seconds, she settled on the evening news. But before she sat down in front of the TV, she bounded up the stairs and checked the answering machine in her office. There were no calls. She was hoping for a message from Jenny. Margaret changed into an old leotard and returned downstairs.

The TV was promptly shut off and replaced by classical music on compact disc. Margaret stretched out on the Soloflex machine in the corner of the living room and began running through her regular routine—some muscle tightening, particularly abdominal muscles. She intended to work out twice a day for the next couple of days, and blow Brian's mind this weekend, maybe.

While running through a repetitive series of crunches, her thoughts drifted to her scheduled luncheon with Reid Birmingham. Was Claire right? Had she made some overwhelming impression on the elegantly handsome lawyer on Tuesday morning or was she getting caught up in one of Claire's melodramas? Margaret became preoccupied with these ideas as she crunched out her repetitions on the Soloflex.

By the clock, Margaret had spent just under thirty minutes on the machine. She worked her abs, backside, thighs and upper body. She concluded the super workout just before eight o'clock and was wearing a thin layer of perspiration over her entire body. As she showered and dressed, she thought about what to wear to the office the next day. Margaret experienced a momentary wave of guilt about her thoughts regarding the luncheon date with Reid, then laughed at herself for constructing something in her head about the lunch. Entering the kitchen, she looked over what she might throw together for dinner. There were enough vegetables to put together a meager salad. That would just have to do, she thought. She was not particularly hungry. The classical CD was beginning to depress her. A shallow, lonely feeling was creeping over her. Margaret decided to call her mom after dinner.

Her salad was nearly prepared when the sound of the phone broke the silence. Anxiously picking up the receiver, she grabbed it before the second ring.

"Olson residence," she answered.

"God, do you sound stuffy when you answer the phone that way." It was Brian.

"It's called refinement, and it's apparently lost on you people from Maine," replied Margaret.

"Don't be so defensive, Keogh. I was just trying to have a little fun with you. I was calling to see how my passion slave was coping with the empty house and all," scoffed Brian.

"Coping's the right word. I'm waiting for a call from my daughter to see how she's doing. Any idea of her whereabouts?" Margaret's voice reflected some agitation.

"I might be able to be of some assistance on the question of your daughter, but I'm disappointed you didn't pick up on the passion slave comment. You're slipping, Keogh. I'm slowly but surely taking full command of this relationship. It's kind of sad watching you concede more and more power to me—very, very, sad." Brian was being Brian, charmingly silly.

"Brian, we both know who the passion slave is. Don't we, Brian? Don't we?" Margaret had changed the tone of her voice to a seductive whisper. "Don't we?" she persisted.

"Yes, master," he conceded jokingly to a chorus of laughter in the background.

"Who's over there with you?" demanded Margaret.

"Your freeloading daughter and her freeloading friend. They stuck me for the check at Felicity's tonight." With that said, Jenny grabbed the phone from Brian and greeted her mother with an enthusiastic gale of house-hunting stories and details from the day's activities. Jenny's voice displayed how excited she was about her first day of independence. This made her mother both happy and disconsolate. Margaret missed Jenny more than she dared admit. Over the next few minutes Margaret outlined instructions regarding mailing addresses, phone numbers, emergency steps in the event of an accident, and a number of additional items of concern to her. Lastly, she told Jenny to go to Brian in the event she could not reach her mother and warned her that she would inspect the cottage in Ogunquit this coming weekend. Finally, Brian wrestled the phone from Jenny and ended the extended mother-daughter conversation.

"You Scottish people really know how to talk when it's someone else's dime," he piped in.

"Thanks for making sure I got to speak to Jenny. It meant a lot."

"Are you okay, Keogh?' asked Brian. He sounded concerned.

"It's just real quiet here, that's all." It was clear to Brian that Margaret was having a difficult time with the empty house. By now Jenny and Trudy had wandered out of the room and he felt free to speak in earnest with her.

"Listen, Maggie, if you want I can come over and spend the night. I could make it there by ten."

"No, it's too far; but thanks for the offer. Hell, I'll be over there Friday night. That'll be soon enough."

"Keogh, just so you know, I'm working a long day tomorrow and opening up Friday morning. All this to justify giving myself the night off. I'll be waiting for you at the cottage Friday night. I've been really missing you lately. I'll be glad when Friday night gets here," he asserted.

"Me, too." Margaret's voice lacked the sincerity of Brian's.

"I love you, Maggie May."

"Ditto," responded Margaret.

"Ditto? What kind of crap is that?" Brian voiced agitation.

"I'm very tired. I'll see you Friday. Good night, Brian." With that, Margaret hung up the phone and returned to the preparation of dinner, which she ate in front of the television set. She retired to her bedroom just before ten o'clock.

14

MARGARET WAS ALREADY AWAKE when her alarm tripped on at six o'clock Thursday morning. The first full night alone in the house had been survived, she thought. She had forgotten, however, to prepare the coffeemaker the night before and became agitated when she arrived in the kitchen to find a cold, empty pot. Jenny had assumed responsibility for the morning coffee after Brad had moved out. Now Margaret realized she would have to fend for herself in the future. She measured out enough ground coffee for a couple of cups and turned on the machine. While it brewed she showered, then went about deciding what to wear. She was already contemplating her lunch with Reid Birmingham and, with due care, reviewing her wardrobe. After two or three aborted decisions she chose a light blue, cotton dress. Margaret had a long-standing fondness for this particular dress because of the way it fit her. It had always clung to her body as if it had been specifically designed for her. It was not even one of her more expensive pieces of clothing. All she knew was that she felt attractive and feminine when she wore it. She saw it in the eyes of people, particularly men, whenever she had it on. She wanted Reid to see her at her best. After twenty minutes in front of the television catching up on the overnight news and weather forecast, she secured the house and drove to the office.

The morning passed slowly with Margaret repeatedly checking the time on her watch. She left word with Gretchen at the front desk to direct Attorney Birmingham to her office upon his arrival. Shortly after 11:30 Margaret became embroiled in a discussion with an employee on the line from Berlin, New Hampshire, an audit site in the northern part of the state. She stood with her back to the door, staring out the window as she spoke. Margaret was reviewing the progress of an audit engagement that was beginning to run over budget, attempting to determine whether she would be forced to spend a day up north in the White Mountains. After bluntly informing her young auditor that it was not in his best interest to require her to join him in Berlin, she ended the conversation with a directive to report back to her on his progress at five o'clock. The conversation over, Margaret turned back to her desk and saw Reid Birmingham standing in the doorway. He wore a wry smile on his face.

"You are a very impressive young businesswoman, Margaret Keogh-Olson."

"Not that young, I'm afraid," she answered modestly.

"A woman in her mid- to late-twenties is young to me," the lawyer replied.

"Counselor, if you're going to shamelessly shower me with compliments, at least make them remotely believable."

"I'm sorry, it must have been your schoolgirl figure that threw me off." He was eyeing Margaret with a flattering stare.

"Nice recovery, counselor, I guess I'll just have to accept the flattery and let it be." Margaret was mildly surprised by the lawyer's demeanor. It appeared Claire could be right. She could clearly see some interest in her coming from him and it was well beyond lawyer-client.

Margaret escorted her guest on a tour of the building, introducing him to members of her staff. She noticed that her female employees, in particular, paid special attention to the handsome attorney. It pleased her that on two occasions Mr. Birmingham complimented her on certain elements of the building's well-preserved colonial interior. She was impressed with how he picked up on subtle details on such a cursory tour. Returning to her corner office, they decided on seafood for lunch. Margaret advised Gretchen that she would be gone for approximately an hour and the couple headed out for their meal.

Attorney Birmingham had walked over to the accounting office, so she drove to the restaurant. The conversation remained light and relaxed during the five-minute ride and remained so while they ordered their meals. After their beverages arrived at the table, Margaret wasted no time directing the conversation toward the exact reason for the meeting.

"So, counselor, I'm more than a little intrigued by your need to speak to me about the divorce. Is this going to be good news or bad news?"

"That's a little hard to say at this point but, first of all, please drop the 'counselor.' It's Reid."

"No nickname? Reido, or Ree for short?" Margaret chuckled as her cavalier attitude seemed to agitate the lawyer slightly.

"No, I'm afraid it's just Reid. It's my mother's maiden name. Anyway, I'm here to ask your permission to refer your case to an associate in the office, Mary Richard. She is tremendously qualified and besides, as you said before, this case is purely administrative. There is nothing to negotiate or contest. It should proceed without a hitch." At this point Margaret's face already reflected her bewilderment.

"I don't understand. Are you saying you're passing on my divorce because it's too small?" she asked.

"No, nothing like that. It's a matter of avoiding anything that could even remotely be construed as a violation of the legal profession's code of ethics," stated the lawyer earnestly.

"I wasn't aware your profession even had a code of ethics," countered Margaret. "But I'm still in the dark here. What exactly are you saying?" She leaned forward, staring directly into the attorney's eyes. The lawyer let out a sigh and broke eye contact. He glanced out the window as if to gather a measure of courage.

"What I am saying so poorly is that I would like to pursue a personal relationship with you, Mrs. Olson, and I would prefer not having even a trace of impropriety involved. That means doing away with the attorney-client relationship. I do hope I'm not talking out of place here. Claire Gagnon gave me the impression that you didn't have anything serious going on at present. Is that correct?" Margaret gave no audible reply but nodded that his information was correct. Now Margaret was quiet, making for an uncomfortable period of silence at the table. She suddenly had to make a snap decision. If her relationship with Brian was to be an exclusive one, then she would have to direct the conversation from its present course. Prompted by his unexpected flattery, Margaret impulsively decided against sending any negative signals toward the attentive lawyer.

"I guess what I'm looking for is a green light to call you in the future. I'm not sure what your interests are, but if we have nothing in common—then I'll adapt," Reid stated modestly.

"Can you play tennis?" she asked.

"You might not want to play tennis with me. I'm pretty good and terribly competitive," boasted Reid.

"I'll be the judge of whether you're pretty good or not, counselor," responded Margaret, a cagey grin crossing her face.

"How about this weekend?" inquired Reid anxiously.

"This weekend's out—prior commitment. Why don't you call me early next week and maybe we can work something out for the following weekend." Reid nodded in agreement as the waitress arrived with their meals. The two spent the next thirty minutes providing each other with details of their lives along with insights into their first impressions of each other from earlier in the week. Margaret withheld expressing her attraction to the good-looking attorney while Reid candidly conceded that he was immediately taken with the attractive accountant.

Following lunch, Margaret drove Reid back to his office. She extended her hand as he exited the car. From the curb, he flashed her a wide grin and called out that he would call her the following week. Margaret returned the smile but hers was more reserved. Driving around the corner to her office, Margaret reflected on an emerging problem. She would have to juggle matters between Brian and her new admirer, but she figured that the distance between Manchester and Wells would work to her advantage. As much as she had enjoyed rekindling the relationship with her high school friend, Margaret realized that she would be insane to simply dismiss the advances of an eligible bachelor with Reid Birmingham's credentials and family background.

15

MARGARET LEFT HER OFFICE in Manchester for the coast of Maine late Friday afternoon. Her car was packed with a fully loaded suitcase. By the time she reached the Maine border, an overcast sky had given way to a steady rain that grew more intense the closer she got to the ocean. Having arrived in Wells by way of Route 1, she turned her BMW onto Mile Road and motored down toward the sea. The car was being buffeted by wind gusts as the rain pounded down on the roof and showered the windshield in sheets. Visibility was poor as Margaret negotiated one turn, then another, until she pulled up to Brian's yellow cottage. His pickup truck was parked out front and she thought she could see him standing on the porch. Waiting a few seconds after turning off the car, she made a quick dash to the front door. It swung open as she reached it, and Brian pulled her in.

"Hey, you made it, and in record time," he said, applying a gentle bear hug on her. "God, Maggie, I've missed you this week," he added.

"I thought you missed me every week?" she replied.

"Well, this week more than usual. I've made us some nice hot chocolate. It'll help thaw you out."

"Jesus, Brian, it's June. The rest of us on planet Earth are not drinking hot chocolate. It's almost summer, for God's sake."

"Hey—Miss Hard Ass, in case you haven't noticed, it's fifty-three degrees out there and you can almost see your breath. Now, are you going to drink my hot chocolate voluntarily or do I have to force it down?" Brian seemed a little put out with Margaret's bitchiness. It seemed less playful and more real than usual.

His guest turned her back and walked to the couch in the corner of the small, enclosed porch. She sat down and looked up at him as if terribly bored.

"I will only drink hot chocolate if I can have marshmallows in it."
She spoke in the forced manner of a spoiled brat.

"I have marshmallows," answered Brian.

"The little ones?" she asked.

"Yes, I have the little ones."

"Is the hot chocolate caffeine-free?" questioned Margaret.

"Do you like it caffeine-free?" asked Brian, now sure she was trying to somehow outwit him.

"Sometimes I like it caffeine-free, and sometimes I like it regular," she retorted, a confident smirk on her face.

"Well, what kind do you think you would like tonight?" Brian asked condescendingly.

"I can't seem to decide. I want to see which one you bring me. Come on, Kelly, get the lead out. Where's my hot chocolate?" She barked out her question and waited for Brian's response. He turned and left the porch without saying a word, then returned from the kitchen in a few seconds with two cups of warm chocolate. Margaret looked up at him as he stood over her with the two cups of steaming beverage.

"Okay, Kelly, which one is mine?" she asked impatiently.

"That depends, Keogh. You see, one cup is regular and one is caffeine-free, and I don't have a preference. So, you take all the time you need to decide because I have both." Brian was beaming, knowing he had outwitted her on this occasion.

"You are so full of shit, Kelly, I can't believe it," she argued, narrowing her eyes as if angry.

"Prove it, Keogh. Prove that both cups are caffeine-free or regular. You can't and you know it!" He jumped down next to Margaret on the couch, pulling her against him. She shifted her head away but he only buried his face in her hair.

"Maggie, I love you so much it's getting hard to be away from you for even a day." His voice contained a serious overtone that warned her that he had lost control of any natural inhibition. His hands turned her face back to him. He kissed her deeply on the mouth. Two weeks earlier this would have inflamed her with passion, but she felt a change. There was no doubt in her mind that Reid Birmingham was the cause. Suddenly Margaret was very afraid of what Brian would say next. She closed her eyes as he continued.

"Maggie, please don't stop me from saying what I'm about to say. If nothing else, it will be very therapeutic. It's just that over the past two months—you have become everything to me. I mean—at some point I realized that there wasn't anything I wouldn't do or give for you. I would die for you. I would hand you over all of my worldly possessions, everything, and not even think twice about it. I love you so much that it scares the hell out of me, because if you can make me this happy, then you can make me just as miserable—if I lost you I mean. And I get no relief from you. The weather comes on TV at night and I see New Hampshire on the map, and I think of you. I see a BMW, any BMW, and I think of you. Someone talks about taxes and I think of you. I get no rest from you. You're always there in my consciousness. I'm saying all this because I want you to know that there are no conditions that I will not meet if you will take me as your husband. I want to marry you because I'm not sure I can continue living without you." As he concluded, Brian appeared emotionally exhausted.

Tears were streaming down her face as Margaret valiantly tried to refrain from sobbing. No one had ever confessed their feelings for her the way Brian had just expressed them. Burying her face into his chest, Margaret began to cry.

"I hope these are tears of joy," he quipped. Brian's voice reflected his anxiety.

"I don't know what to say. It's really overwhelming." Margaret knew she could not accept this proposal from Brian. She had just discovered Reid. Abandoning that budding relationship, and the tremendous potential that went with it, was out of the question. For a brief moment she even resented him for caring so much.

"Brian, you know I love you and love being with you, but I'm not as emotional as you. I will need more time to think everything through," she confessed. Margaret decided to bide for time and draw back from the situation at hand. "There are a million considerations involved here. Who moves where? And how about prenuptial agreements and the like? It isn't as simple as just saying 'yes' and doing it." She locked eyes with him, searching for a clue to how he was accepting her reaction.

"I've already told you I'll concede on every point and issue, but I'm not going to try to force this down your throat. I love you, and I'm willing to wait if that's what it takes," offered Brian. Margaret responded with an understanding smile. She was anxious to change the mood and subject of the conversation.

"So, Kelly, what do you have planned for the evening?" she asked lightheartedly.

"See how this sounds, Maggie May. I take you up to Kennebunkport for dinner. There's a restaurant up there with this really inexperienced waitress, a real basket case. Has a New Hampshire accent—a real screw-up. The kid can't be more than eighteen years old—looks a little like you come to think of it. She could be your sister. She's prettier than you though. Anyway, why don't we go up there and ask to be seated at one of her tables? We'll drive her nuts! We'll complain about everything! How does that sound?" Margaret knew immediately that Brian planned to bring her to wherever Jenny was working. This pleased her immensely.

"Will you help me unload my car?" she asked in her most pathetic voice. Brian propped her back on the couch.

"Drink your hot chocolate," he instructed. Seconds later he was bounding out to the BMW while the blowing rain washed over him.

* * *

Brian and an thoroughly exhausted Margaret visited Jenny at Dunbar's, a trendy eatery just steps from Dock Square in Kennebunkport. True to his word, he managed to get them seated at one of Jenny's tables. She was overjoyed to see her mother and updated her on everything that had happened since her arrival in Maine. Following dinner, Brian brought an emotionally drained Margaret to Wells Beach, convincing her to join him for a walk along the churning ocean. The rain had tapered off to a foggy mist. The ocean air was raw but invigorating as Margaret and Brian tried to walk off the effects of a heavy meal. Returning to the cozy, warm cottage on the estuary, Brian attempted, unsuccessfully, to introduce romance into the evening's proceedings. Instead, Margaret propped herself up in bed and used Brian's TV remote to channel surf through the cable stations. She did not resist when Brian began to knead her neck and shoulder muscles. Instead, she stretched out and ridiculed the quality of programming available on television. She nodded off after twenty minutes of serious massage. The ocean air provided her with the ingredients for a deep, restful sleep. When Margaret awoke at eight o'clock the next morning, she was alone in bed. Brian had left for the lodge earlier and had not awakened her.

Margaret pampered herself by staying in bed until well after nine o'clock. Awakening with little appetite, she prepared only a half-pot of coffee and emerged from the cottage onto the deck with a cup of her standard brew, extra cream, no sugar. She collapsed onto one of four chairs, propping her bare feet up onto the sturdy deck railing. The air was fresh from the effects of the heavy rain the night before, while the estuary grass glistened from some of its remaining moisture. Margaret methodically sipped on the hot coffee, taking time to savor the rich blend. She thought of what a contrast this was from her coffee-drinking routine in the office.

Eventually she rose to her feet and slowly walked around the grassy lot. She estimated it was approximately 100 by 100 feet, a large lot by Wells Beach standards. She marveled at the unobstructed view of the estuary and wildlife sanctuary in three directions. She tried to approximate its value. Margaret settled on between $100,000 and $150,000 for the land and maybe another $50,000 for the building. Strolling back toward the rustic storage shed at the edge of the property, she eyed Brian's canoe. He had taken her for a ride during her first visit but not since that time. After only moments of indecision, she swallowed the remainder of her coffee and strode over to the boat. It was usually locked with a chain, but Margaret saw that on this day it was unsecured. Thankful for her good fortune, she removed one of the paddles from the shed and slowly lugged the canoe across the yard to the edge of the water. The tide was perfect for a launch and, within seconds, she was cautiously paddling her way through the fifteen-foot-wide passageway toward more open water.

Margaret trusted her instincts as she maneuvered the canoe farther and farther from the cottage. The estuary had no vegetation except for the long marsh grass that laid flat on the ground. She was able to keep her bearings at all times by observing where she was in relation to Brian's cottage. Margaret had paddled for only a few minutes when she was overcome by the beauty of her surroundings. Putting her paddle down inside the canoe, she listened to the sound of the clear, blue water wash up against its side.

The rhythmic sound of the water against the side of the canoe was so restful Margaret was tempted to lie down and just drift. She did not, however; instead she chose to consider the difficult decisions her actions were directing her toward. Without question, Reid Birmingham was undermining her feelings for Brian. Reid was invading her thoughts during the day and inciting emotional stirrings in her at night. Only a fool would try to deny the feelings he was bringing about in her. Margaret contemplated whether she would be able to keep Brian at bay for a time while she explored her passion for Reid. Thoughts of a possible relationship with Reid swept over her as she drifted on the estuary. Laying her hand over the side of the canoe, Margaret dropped it into the clean saltwater. The cold water temperature brought her out of her thoughts and back to the situation at hand. Looking back to the cottage she saw someone standing at the edge of his property. She strained her eyes, lifting her hand to block the sun's rays. It was Brian.

She picked up the paddle and reluctantly began paddling the canoe back toward the house. Brian's eyes were locked on her as she deliberately maneuvered through a short series of passageways on the estuary. Margaret became aware of an unpleasant emotion growing in her. As the boat glided nearer to Brian, she realized that she resented him. She resented this disturbance during her peaceful interlude on the water. She resented Brian for keeping her from Reid this weekend. But, more than anything, she resented him for loving her more than she wanted to be loved. With the canoe gliding toward the edge of his property, Margaret tried to conceal these feelings.

"What are you doing out on the water without a life jacket?" Brian asked, plainly concerned.

"They're too restrictive," she snapped back.

"Restrictive or not, the next time I catch you out there without a life jacket, I'm taking you over my knee," said Brian kiddingly.

"Lay a hand on me and it'll be the last thing you ever do with me!"

"Jesus, Keogh, lighten up." Cupping his hands over her head he pulled her face to face with him.

"I was just kidding with you, or trying to. I love seeing you enjoying yourself, but next time, bring along something for floatation in case of an accident, okay?"

Margaret did not answer him. Instead, she walked past him across the lawn to the house.

"I'm afraid I have some lousy news for you, Maggie. I was counting on Hal to sub for me the rest of the day but that's out. It seems he was in a car accident last night and bumped his head pretty good, which means I'm going to have to go back to the lodge in about an hour and work right through." Brian's face betrayed his disappointment.

"What? Millie can't work for you?" responded Margaret dourly.

"She's got the afternoon and evening off to go to a wedding. She's at the lodge now but only 'til noon."

"Maybe I should just go home and get some badly needed work done," snapped Margaret, rising from her chair and striding to the front door. Brian caught her at the doorway.

"Why the hell are you acting this way? I didn't plan this to happen. Maggie, lighten up." He whispered the last two words to remove the edge from his voice. "Okay Keogh, listen closely to what I'm about to say. If you will entertain yourself for the rest of the day, when I come back and join you later tonight, I will administer pleasure upon your magnificent body the likes of which you cannot even begin to imagine. You see, I've been holding back something so pleasurable that one woman in ten is said to go stark raving mad by its conclusion. All you have to do is amuse yourself for the rest of the day and this will be performed on you in this very house. Is it a deal, Keogh?"

"I'll see how I feel later," answered Margaret unenthusiastically.

Margaret and Brian spent their remaining time together exchanging small talk and drinking coffee. Margaret did not bring up her plans for the following weekend. There was also no mention of Brian's proposal of marriage the preceding day. Offhandedly, she spoke of her pending divorce and the financial arrangement that she had reached with Brad.

Brian returned to the Atlantic Coast Lodge at a few minutes before noon. Margaret drove north and treated Jenny and Trudy to lunch in Kennebunkport. It was just after three o'clock, back in the cottage, when Margaret then decided to return early to New Hampshire. After scribbling a note and posting it on Brian's refrigerator door, she put the last of her things in the BMW and drove away from the cottage.

* * *

It was a busy day for Brian. The rooms in the lodge had been reserved for over a month, but many of the cottages and a few motel units remained vacant well into the afternoon. Things picked up after 3:00 and by 6:30 he was able to stroll out to Route 1 and hang the "no" in front of the "vacancy" on the large sign. With the last unit rented, he began attending to the needs and questions of his guests in the complex. Recommending restaurants, both good and inexpensive, suggesting local entertainment which included live theater, a drive-in movie, miniature golf courses and pubs—Brian did all of this with the enthusiasm of a schoolboy. He even directed guests to a pub a few miles north of Wells that publicized the presence of an active ghost on the premises. This was the part of his job that he truly loved, the interaction with the visitors. A lull fell over the complex just after 11:30. This was his cue to hand over the front desk to a young, part-time assistant and leave for home. Millie was coming in early the next morning so Brian was covered until three the following afternoon. Hopping into the Ford, he sped down Mile Road toward the ocean. It was 1.4 miles from the entrance of Atlantic Coast Lodge to his front door. A jolt of despair hit him as he approached the cottage and saw no BMW parked out front.

Throughout the weekend Brian had sensed a problem with Maggie but he had tried to dismiss it. Now he was stepping inside a dark house that only five minutes earlier held the promise of romantic and sexual bliss for him. For a split second Brian thought Margaret might be hiding somewhere, waiting to pounce on him. He was quick to reject that notion. It was not her way. It was his way, but not hers. Brian flipped the kitchen light switch and immediately spotted the note scrawled in Margaret's handwriting.

Brian,

Had too many things going on back home and had to get back. Sorry about the lack of warning. I'll speak to you during the week.

Margaret

Brian slumped down into the only chair in his living room. He internalized all of the possible motives that might have caused Margaret to retreat back to New Hampshire. Tonight he would not let his heart hear what his more logical mind was poised to tell it. He would give Maggie the benefit of the doubt, for the sake of his own peace of mind. A half hour passed before he retired to the bedroom. He was thinking of an old-timer he had gotten to know at the pub a few years earlier. Brian had gone to the man's funeral at St. Mary's less than six months ago. Brian remembered seeking his counsel near the end of a particularly painful summer romance. This elderly fellow had told Brian that when you were in love, you often doubted what you most believed. The words had stayed with him.

* * *

The driving time to Bedford was ninety minutes and Margaret decided to put it to good use. With the radio turned off and all her cassette tapes crammed into the glove compartment, she devoted her complete attention to the problem at hand. First she established the given: she had already decided to pursue the budding relationship with Reid. He had the business and social contacts to elevate her to another level in life—professionally and personally. In addition, he was personable, educated, great looking and was clearly on a fast track in his career. The difficulty surrounding her otherwise enviable situation was in the person of Brian Kelly.

Margaret reasoned that if her relationship with Brian was to survive, he would somehow have to be kept inconspicuous so that it would not come to Reid's attention. It helped that Brian was more than an hour's drive away in Maine so that he and Reid were not likely to bump into each other. However, she knew from the present state of their relationship that Brian was not about to give her a six-month leave of absence. And she had complicated matters by assuring Reid that there was no one else in her life. If Reid were to find out about Brian, not only would she be trapped in a lie, but the psychological advantage, which she seemed to hold over the lawyer would surely vanish.

Margaret felt increasingly frustrated as she attempted to think of a creative but believable set of circumstances under which she could put her relationship with Brian on hold. She found it bitterly ironic that he would propose marriage on the eve of her decision to downgrade their relationship, at least temporarily. The thought of hurting Brian was beginning to depress her. Perhaps in self-defense, she began to rationalize her actions during the past two months and the role that he could have played in a deteriorating situation. Margaret reasoned that her trip to Wells after tax season was planned solely to apologize for the oversight on her part years before, and that the affair that resulted was largely triggered by Brian's attention to her. For all she knew, Brian could have lured any number of women to his bed with the same casual charm and the promise of a capable massage.

As Margaret continued to mull over her circumstances, she turned her attention to a financial reality. Brian was a fractional owner of a quaint, apparently successfully, vacation complex. At best, Brian represented a lateral move from her soon-to-be ex-husband. He did not appear to have the education or drive to dramatically improve his financial prospects. Did it make sense for her to even seriously consider the marriage option now, or even in the future? She cared for Brain deeply, but she was still willing to pursue the new man in her life, and that had to mean something. She felt dispirited.

As her BMW sped over the Merrimack River and entered Bedford, Margaret came up with a strategy. She would force Brian to the back of her mind. She would not contact him for a time—perhaps frustrate and anger him to the extent that he would call an end to things. If he broke off the relationship, she would be spared the pain of doing it. She reasoned that it would be easier to crawl back to Brian, if need be, than to confront him with her intention to cool things down while she explored a relationship with another man. A weak, half-baked strategy is better than none at all, she thought, as the car rolled up the driveway in front of her house.

Before unpacking the car or even opening a window, Margaret marched up the stairway to her office and checked for phone messages. There was single blinking light to signify one message. She hit the rewind button and listened. It was a long rewind, meaning a long message. Margaret hit "play," and after the beep she heard:

"Hello, Margaret, it's Reid. I called on the faint hope that your plans could have been canceled or changed. I guess not. If you get in at a respectable time on Sunday night, would you give me a ring? I'm assuming you still have my number. Oh, I spoke to Claire about you. I saw her at the health club. She says you're quite a tennis player. I just want to remind you that steamrollering over other women is one thing, beating me will be a whole different matter. Hope to hear from you."

Margaret smiled as she rewound the tape. She was delighted that Reid had not been able to resist calling her, even over the weekend. She briefly considered returning his call but decided against it. She had the upper hand. He was very interested. She would do nothing to jeopardize her advantage. Margaret had already concluded that she should continue to be aloof around the attorney. She decided to make him call her with a follow-up. She was on top in this mind game with the handsome lawyer and she knew it. All she had to do was remain strong. Margaret planned to keep her distance and maintain full control of the relationship. If she understood male psychology, and she thought she did, this would only heighten Reid Birmingham's interest in her.

Margaret prepared herself a light dinner from the refrigerator, caught up on some technical reading, and retired to bed early on Saturday night. The phone message gave her a pleasant feeling and she ran it over in her mind as she fell asleep.

16

MARGARET WAS FIRST TO ARRIVE at the office Monday morning. She had spent the better part of Sunday working at home on general, administrative matters that required minimal thought. The simple content of her workload allowed her to monitor the political analysis programs telecast throughout the morning and afternoon. Repeatedly, Margaret had thought of Reid and her probable date with him the following weekend. She had also thought of Brian. Margaret had envisioned his return to the empty cottage and his reaction to her cryptic note. This image was producing continuing feelings of discomfort.

These thoughts still streamed through her consciousness as she sat at her desk Monday morning. Her mind focused as a call was transferred to her office.

"Margaret Olson," she answered in her standard, monotone voice.

"Hello, Mrs. Olson, it's your former attorney getting in touch as promised. I decided not to sit around all day waiting for you to call me."

"Very wise decision, counselor. It would have been a long, long wait," she snapped back.

"I wanted to make it onto your social calendar before it was totally booked. How about this—I'll spring for lunch on Thursday and at that time we can finalize plans for tennis on the weekend. If you have no problem with it, I'd love to take you over to my folk's place at Dover Point. They've got a court out back where we can slug it out without an audience."

"Why should an audience bother you, counselor? You aren't losing any of that male confidence are you?" quizzed Margaret light-heartedly.

"God, I'm going to enjoy bringing you down a few pegs," he said.

"What time for lunch on Thursday?" she asked impatiently.

"Are you pressed for time?" he asked.

"Always."

"Noon, okay?" he offered.

"Consider it a date. Pick me up here. Good-bye, counselor," said Margaret, hanging up the phone before he could respond.

Walking around her desk and out into the hall, Margaret chuckled a little to herself. Her plan was to keep Reid Birmingham completely off balance. The preceding phone conversation did nothing to undermine her strategy. She descended the stairs and approached Gretchen at the front desk.

"Gretchen, until further notice I want all of my calls screened. Continue to use your best judgment on them but I don't wish to speak to Brian Kelly under any circumstances. Just indicate that I'm out of the office and take a message. Is that clear?"

The pretty, young receptionist nodded yes and returned to work. Margaret was burdened with the knowledge that Brian would be trying to contact her. She knew there was going to be a confrontation of some sort and she dreaded the prospect of it.

After closing out two productive days at the office, Margaret closed the door behind her on Tuesday night and made her way back to her empty house. Jenny's absence and the pending turnover of men in her life was good cause to immerse herself in her work. At present, she was monitoring two of Vern Butler's major clients along with her own workload. The Butlers were vacationing in Canada for the next two weeks, placing the extra burden on her.

On the commute home it struck her how bright the sky remained beyond eight o'clock in the evening. It was nearly summer and almost the longest day of the year. As she drove home to Bedford, personal matters came to mind. Jenny had not called in three days, so Margaret decided to call her daughter that evening. The BMW rolled to a stop at the front door and her white, colonial home loomed in front of her, quiet and empty. Margaret reminded herself that tomorrow night Claire would be staying over. This cheered her. It would be good having her friend for dinner to help break the silence which now seemed to literally inhabit her home.

Margaret entered the front door and routinely climbed the stairs to her bedroom. She would make herself comfortable before preparing dinner. Peeking through the door of her home office she saw the message light on the answering machine flashing. One flash—one message. She walked over and rewound the incoming tape. It was a long message. She pressed "play." Her stomach knotted at the sound of Brian Kelly's voice.

"Dammit, Maggie, what's going on? I thought I'd have heard from you by now." Brian's voice was flat and sluggish. "When you left that way over the weekend I thought you might be sick or something. If it has to do with the proposal, well, if I'm scaring you or something then we'll just put everything on hold. I don't want to rush things if it's that. This probably isn't making too much sense. God, I hate talking into machines, but I really need to speak to you, kid. I don't know what's going on! Please get back to me tonight. I'm at the lodge. You have the number." Brian paused and let out a sigh. "Please get back to me tonight. I mean I'm starting to imagine all sorts of crazy stuff. Okay, Keogh? Oh, it's five past six." Then came the click of the discontinued call.

For a moment Margaret considered picking up the phone and calling him back. Brian sounded very troubled. She asked herself what she could say to make him feel better. Anything she could say would just be painful. Margaret tried comforting herself by theorizing that Brian might come to the conclusion she was out of town and not returning his call for that reason. Margaret knew she lacked the courage to return his call, at least this evening. She told herself that she might have the courage tomorrow night with Claire on hand for moral support. Forcing Brian out of her mind for the moment, she rang Jenny's cottage. Nine rings later she hung up the phone, vowing to bring her daughter an answering machine on her next visit to Maine.

Margaret forced herself onto the Soloflex machine for fifteen minutes of strenuous work before preparing dinner. She was already thinking about her tennis match with Reid on Saturday. Maybe Claire could play a couple of sets with her on Wednesday after work? That would help keep her ground strokes sharp for the weekend. Her mind continued to randomly consider these matters as she picked at her dinner while seated in front of the television. She tried, unsuccessfully, to reach Jenny one more time before retiring for the evening.

* * *

Claire met Margaret at the club after work on Wednesday. They managed to squeeze in two sets of tennis in an hour's time. Margaret, employing her no-nonsense approach to the game, dispatched of Claire in straight sets, 6-0 and 6-2. The two friends decided to go directly back to Bedford after completing play. They wanted to shower in Bedford at Margaret's house in comfortable surroundings. Margaret had picked up Claire at her office before going to the club and so they traveled together in the BMW. Margaret made it known that she was thrilled to have Claire as a houseguest for the night, while Claire seemed happy to spend some personal time with her closest friend.

They had showered and were busy preparing a salad of fresh vegetables and fruit when Margaret brought up the delicate situation involving her and Brian.

"I hope you don't mind but I was hoping to use you as a sounding board regarding my situation with Brian."

"You know, I haven't said anything about Brian to you but I have to admit I've been curious. How much have you told him about Reid?" asked Claire. Margaret's face turned more serious.

"Nothing, absolutely nothing." Margaret paused as she struggled to share her emotions. "Last weekend Brian asked me to marry him."

"And what did you say?" asked Claire, dumbfounded, because she didn't know there was anything serious between Margaret and Brian.

" I didn't give him an answer. I came home early over the weekend, while he was at work. We haven't spoken since then. I just don't know what to tell him. I know I can't marry him with everything breaking the way it is with Reid and all. Jesus, Claire, if you could've heard what he said to me when he proposed." Margaret's eyes were filling up as she fought with her emotions.

"What did he say?" asked Claire, now emerged in her friend's situation.

"It wasn't just what he said, but the way he said it. He was so honest with me about how he felt. He's always been that way. He told me he'd do anything for me—anything, and I know he meant it literally, not figuratively. He feels things more deeply than me—more than most people do." She dropped her eyes down to a kitchen counter scattered with partially prepared vegetables.

"He's already called the house once looking for me. I sort of left things up in the air when I left over the weekend. Damn it! If I'd known I'd be meeting someone like Reid, there's no way I would have let things go so far with him."

"It's twenty-twenty you know," quipped Claire.

"What is?" asked Margaret.

"Hindsight," answered Claire while reaching over and giving her friend a reassuring squeeze. "If there's anything I can do to help, just ask. Do you understand? Just ask. If you don't mind a little advice then I would suggest you get back to Brian and not leave him in the dark." Claire looked over at Margaret for a hint to what she might be thinking. "If you call him tonight, at least you'll have me for emotional support," added Claire.

"I was thinking of writing him a long letter to tell him what's happened."

Claire grimaced. "It wouldn't be my first choice. Would it really be that hard to just call and break the news?"

"I just can't. I hate things like this. I have no stomach for interpersonal confrontations. Make it business and I love it—I thrive on it. But this sort of thing comes along and I'm an emotional wreck." Margaret stopped for a moment, and after recovering her composure, calmly resumed speaking.

"Claire, if I had more than one life to give, I'd give one of those lives to Brian Kelly, but Reid is everything I've ever wanted," admitted Margaret. She was being uncharacteristically emotional. Claire saw the conversation beginning to take its toll on her friend and jumped on an opportunity to change the subject.

"By the way, thank you for taking it easy on me in the second set tonight. You're playing very well right now." Margaret cracked a weak smile.

"I know a certain lawyer who had better not take his match with a girl too lightly," mused Margaret.

The women finished preparing dinner, filled a pair of glass flutes with imported white wine, and dined outside on the patio. The evening air was ideal as they discussed everything and anything except business and romantic complications.

Claire's overnight stay provided Margaret with a much-needed emotional lift, and a call from Jenny the same evening helped her look forward to the second half of the week. Lunch with Reid went off without a hitch and plans were solidified for tennis on Saturday morning. It was agreed that he would pick Margaret up at her house and drive to Dover Point on New Hampshire's Great Bay. There, they would play on a private court behind his parents' home. Margaret was curious to see how the fourth-richest family in the state lived.

On Thursday night Margaret sat down and wrote a short letter to Brian that would close the second chapter in her life in which he had played a major part.

> *Brian,*
>
> *You must believe me when I tell you that writing this letter is one of the most difficult things I have ever had to do. There is no good way to say what has to be said. I cannot accept your marriage proposal, although I am very*

flattered to have received it. What's more, it is my feeling that we should discontinue seeing each other. Recently, I met someone who has had a profound effect on me. Any continued involvement with you could only undermine this new relationship in my life. I know nothing I write or say could possibly eliminate the disappointment that this probably brings you. I only hope that you will understand why I must do this at this time. I sincerely wish you the very best of everything from the bottom of my heart.

    Margaret

She mailed the letter at the Bedford Post Office on Friday morning. For the rest of the day she was plagued with the image of Brian reading it on the front porch of the cottage. She consoled herself with the thought that it had been a relationship doomed to failure from day one. Margaret reasoned that going to Maine, and looking up Brian Kelly, had been a mistake. It had been brought about by her loneliness. Hopefully, he would recover quickly from this whole, misguided affair, she thought. She drew additional consolation from the fact that Brian was strong, in spite of his sometimes sophomoric behavior. She was convinced that he would be okay. In fact, she was sure of it. Brian was a survivor.

17

MARGARET ROSE EARLY SATURDAY MORNING, six o'clock to be precise. Reid was picking her up at nine but she planned to begin
preparing for her tennis match much earlier. By 6:45 she was at the
elementary school, working on her ground strokes against the wall of
the building. She would often go out and practice her serve and ground
strokes before a tennis match, particularly before playing a difficult
opponent. Margaret felt strongly about playing well against Reid and
had decided to use her favorite ploy. This involved practicing her game
before a match, then dissuading her opponent from warming up under
the pretense that both would be equally impacted by the lack of practice strokes. If her opponent agreed to her suggestion, and they usually did, she would roar into the lead as a result of her pre-match warm-
up. Margaret firmly believed in grabbing any advantage available to
her, whether on business or personal matters.

Arriving back at the house after a solid forty-five minutes of practice at the wall, she showered, prepared coffee, and listened to the
latest weather forecast on the cable channel. She was seated on the
patio when Reid's Porsche pulled into the driveway.

He dropped the sunglasses from his eyes as Margaret walked toward the car dressed in her tennis whites. Her skirt helped to showcase
her shapely, tan, athletic legs to their fullest. She smiled as she reached
the car, tossing her travel bag and racket into the back of the vehicle.

"I hope you thought to bring a swimsuit with you. We can hit the
pool after we're through playing," he said.

Margaret nodded yes. "I was hoping we could find some water
somewhere after a few sets. You'll probably think I'm prudish once
you see the suit," she added.

The cool morning air was already beginning to give way to a fiery
summer sun as they sped eastward. The conversation was relaxed and

unforced as Reid drove along Route 101 toward the Atlantic. From time to time Margaret noticed the attorney's eyes shifting downward, almost involuntarily, to her outstretched legs as he routinely glanced over at her. It worked out well for her if Attorney Birmingham was a "leg" man. She laughed to herself from the knowledge that she may have the ability to keep his interest with or without her mind games.

Following forty minutes on primary roads, Reid directed the car along a secondary road, affording Margaret her first glimpse of Great Bay on this day. The sun was rising higher into the sky, sending streams of golden light reflecting off the water. The air outside the car looked heavy. Margaret thought back to the weather forecast from an hour earlier—hot and humid across New Hampshire with temperatures in the mid-nineties. There were even warnings for people to take it easy, maybe stay near an air conditioner. Reid spoke, breaking her train of thought.

"Well, we're here." He turned the Porsche into the driveway between two granite columns and proceeded along a roadway flanked on both sides by a meticulously groomed lawn. Before Margaret was the main house, a grand building that had her conjuring up images of the mansions in Newport. The house lacked the size of those Rhode Island mansions but did project a measure of their majesty. Margaret did not speak as the car rolled to a halt at the front door.

"The tennis court is out back," Reid said, reaching into the back of the car and grabbing all of their gear. They let out a simultaneous groan as the doors of the Porsche opened and the hot, humid air rushed in. Reid walked around to the passenger side of the vehicle, directing Margaret over the lawn to the far side of the house. There she saw a single tennis court perched at the crest of a sloping hill running down to Great Bay. About thirty yards from the court was a green-tiled, kidney-shaped swimming pool complete with dressing room.

"We don't have to go far for that swim," stated Reid, a proud grin covering his face. It was clear to him that his guest was impressed with the Birmingham estate.

"I guess not," replied Margaret, somewhat taken aback by the surrounding trappings of wealth. They walked together to the tennis court gate, which he politely opened for her.

"What do you say, Martina, best two out of three sets?" he asked. Margaret merely smirked at his weak attempt at humor.

"Best two out of three! You're not going to wimp out on me, counselor, are you? You're not playing with the sissy boys at the club, you're playing with me. How about best three out of five?"

Reid looked at her in disbelief, then began shaking his head. "You're a real piece of work, Mrs. Olson. Okay, as you wish, best three out of five."

Following his concession, Margaret began explaining to the attorney how they might forego the customary warm-up period and just begin play. She reasoned that they probably would be playing for an extended time as it was, and they could simply play themselves into the match. Reid agreed, and with little more than a handful of practice serves the two began their long-awaited match under a sun that was already beginning to bake the New Hampshire landscape.

The benefits from Margaret's strategy were short-lived. After winning the first two games, she experienced great difficulty returning the lawyer's strong serve. At the same time, her own serve was not up to par, enabling the lawyer to take the next five games. She was making him work hard for every point, but his serve and volley tactics were working nonetheless. After stopping his run of five straight games by holding her own serve, Reid held serve himself and won the first set, 6-3.

"For a woman, you're a damn good tennis player," he called across the court to her. Margaret gestured back in a polite manner and glanced down at her watch. The first set had taken forty minutes, thanks to a number of long rallies. Reid's shirt was already soaking wet from the heat and humidity.

"I'm going up to the house and get a pitcher of water. Can I get you one?" he called across the court.

"Yes, please. Just don't take too much time, counselor, I'm just getting warmed up." The attorney turned and slowly climbed the grassy hill to the house. Margaret took this opportunity to look around the grounds. She had expected to be impressed when she accepted Reid's invitation to play at his folk's house, but this was even more than she had imagined. Glancing over her shoulder, she looked out over the bay which touched the edge of the property, roughly a hundred yards away. A single yacht lay anchored a few hundred feet offshore. She tried to imagine the kind of life this level of luxury afforded Reid as he was growing up. Then her mind strayed; she thought of her daughter up in Maine. Thinking about Jenny, she wondered how she was holding up under the strain of long hours and crabby customers in Kennebunkport. Margaret thought about the letter she mailed off to Brian Friday morning. She wondered if he had received it by now. The slam of a door from the house brought her out of her daydream as she caught sight of Reid carrying two containers of water back to the court.

After thanking him for bringing her water, Margaret took a single swallow and immediately raced back onto the court.

"It's my serve," she announced, prompting Reid to put down his pitcher of water and take up his racket. The second set found Margaret changing strategy. In the first set she had attempted to rally forehand to forehand with her male opponent. She now decided to employ a more conservative game plan by returning his shots with high, arching moonballs in an attempt to lengthen the time required to complete a game. This strategy also had a tendency to frustrate a free-swinging, power player like Reid. For the next forty-five minutes the two played on even terms. The score of the second set was tied at four games each when Margaret thought she detected a change in the attorney's play. First, he was slow to react to a forehand down the line, resulting in an easy point for her. On the following point, her serve went down the line for an ace, her first of the day. Margaret's spirits began to soar. Reid was beginning to run down like an old clock, she thought.

"Four serving five, counselor. Don't go and lose the next game or this match is all even," chided Margaret, her confidence beginning to brim over.

The lawyer's face turned more serious as he deliberated prior to the next game. By now his shirt was wringing wet and his face clearly showed the effects of the ninety-degree heat. His first serve landed a foot down in the net and Margaret drove his second, controlled serve down the line for a winner. Following that, he proceeded to double fault away the next two points. His back to the wall, Reid managed to put his next serve in play, only to have Margaret drive it right back at him on a line. Margaret won the point and the second set, 6-4.

They met at the bench for a short rest between sets. Margaret toweled herself while Reid gulped down most of the remaining water in his bottle. For her part, Margaret took a quick swig from her bottle and ran back out onto the court.

"Don't forget, counselor, best three out of five," she heckled.

Reid methodically rose from the bench and walked back onto the court. It was evident to Margaret that he was somewhere between tired and exhausted. She was feeling the heat herself but was convinced she could outlast her handsome opponent if the match managed to drag on. Margaret took the first game of the third set without losing a point. Then, having no problem returning Reid's serve, took game two after five, long, grueling points. After that, the lawyer walked slowly back to the bench and sat down.

"Do you mind sharing some of your water?" he asked.

"No, go ahead," sang out Margaret. He lifted the water bottle, taking a couple of mouthfuls. He poured the rest over his head as he slumped down onto the concrete, breathing heavily through his mouth.

"I'm through for the day," he called out, sounding fatigued.

Margaret walked over to him, tossing her racket into her traveling bag. Then, she stunned him by collapsing onto his lap. For a moment he could only stare at her.

"Does that mean you'll take me swimming now?" she asked in her well-rehearsed, Shirley Temple voice. Reid burst out laughing, while perspiration ran down his flushed face.

"May I tell you something, Margaret Keogh-Olson?" he asked.

"Go ahead, I'm tough, I can take it," she responded.

"You're the girl of my dreams. I never knew anyone like you could ever exist. You—are—incredible!" he said methodically.

"Maybe you'd better hold off on all this praise until you see me in my bathing suit," she answered, flattered by his declaration.

"There is no way you could look anything but spectacular with this pair of legs," Reid exclaimed. Margaret blushed slightly.

"Just one more thing, counselor. Are you proud of me, I mean, now that I've whipped your sorry ass?" The lawyer threw his arms around her, kissing her for the first time. Their tired, perspiring bodies remained against each other as they experienced their first intimate moments. They languished in each other's arms for the next few minutes, only a handful of words being spoken. Finally, Reid lifted Margaret's head from his chest.

"I could go for that swim about now. How about you?" he asked. Margaret agreed and the two picked up their gear and walked toward the pool.

"You know Margaret, I knew the match was over when you took the second set," stated Reid.

"Counselor, it was over a lot earlier than that," she came back.

"Meaning what?" asked Reid, puzzled by her response.

"Reid—Reid—Reid. I knew the outcome the moment you let me pressure you into five sets. Think it through! I'm the exercise junkie who runs five times a week, works out at the club when she doesn't run and watches television from her Soloflex at night. It's ninety-five degrees and as humid as hell. There was no way you were going to take three sets from me before the weather got to you! You've got to remember, tennis is a physical game of chess. It's half mental, and you weren't thinking, counselor." Margaret reached over and squeezed his chin as she finished disclosing her strategy.

"Remind me never to underestimate you again," he added sheepishly as they reached the gate to the pool area.

They changed into bathing suits in adjoining bathhouse rooms and met back at the shallow end of the pool. Margaret wore a conservative, forest green, one-piece suit that, nonetheless, showcased her fine-tuned athletic body. Reid wore loose-fitting trunks that complemented his reasonably fit physique. Following the initial shock of the cool water on their warm bodies, the two played together above and below the water's surface. Margaret was pleased that Reid's defeat at tennis had no noticeable effect on his disposition. On no less than three occasions he swam over and kissed her. He also took the opportunity to innocently touch her body more than once while maneuvering his way by her. After thoroughly cooling off in the pool, they rested on adjoining lounges while the sun continued to bake everything under it. From their vantage point it was possible to look out over Great Bay and watch some of the boating activity in the distance. Margaret's curiosity finally prompted her to speak.

"I notice there's a fairly large boat anchored off your shoreline."

"Yes, that's my dad's pride and joy. That yawl's a fifty-footer he picked up just after the recession kicked in. He won't tell anyone what he paid for it, but I get the impression he practically stole it. He hasn't had it that long," added Reid.

"By the way, where are your parents? I'd love to meet them," exclaimed Margaret.

"They're on Martha's Vineyard for the weekend. We have a summer home there and they try to spend as much time there as they can."

Throughout the afternoon Margaret and Reid escaped the oppressive heat by taking extended dips in the water. They made a game of assisting each other in applying sun block lotion to all areas of exposed skin. Margaret was pleased as their relationship seemed to grow more comfortable with each passing hour. Following an extended drying-off period out of the pool, Reid invited her up to the house. If the outside of the Birmingham residence had impressed Margaret, the inside, with its fine quality furnishings and sweeping architectural layout, proved no less splendid. By her count, there were eighteen rooms, including a private library so grand that Margaret asked Reid to allow her to view it a second time at the conclusion of her tour. Reid was not simply impressing Margaret, he was dazzling her. Even his boyhood bedroom reminded her of layouts found in stylish magazine articles.

Upon completing their tour of the house, Reid asked Margaret if she would be interested in taking the dinghy out to his father's yacht.

Margaret accepted the invitation and a few minutes later he was rowing them toward the two-masted ship. Once on deck, he explained a few of the technical elements that made up the nautical gear and rigging while Margaret listened politely. However, it was not until he took her below deck to the sleeping quarters that Margaret was able to fully appreciate the vessel for what it was. The yacht was an extension of the Birmingham's home on the water.

By the time Reid began rowing the two back to shore, Margaret was beginning to feel intimidated by what she saw. She had expected to be impressed by the Birmingham family's possessions, but not overwhelmed. Margaret had been around the wealthy before, assisting them on financial and tax matters. Nevertheless, this was different. This was personal and the Birmingham's almost seemed like something from an F. Scott Fitzgerald novel. They had reached shore and started up the hill when Reid reached over and squeezed Margaret's hand.

"Don't take this the wrong way but, I wonder if I could convince you to stay the night?" he asked almost apologetically.

"Meaning what?" questioned Margaret.

"Meaning you stay in the guest room, which has a lock, and I'll fix breakfast for you in the morning," replied the attorney.

"Guest room? Counselor, I counted six guest rooms," she said laughingly. Reid seemed relieved that Margaret was not insulted.

"Take whichever one you want," he offered.

Margaret and Reid spent most of the evening cuddled together in front of his folks' wide screen television. After reviewing his parents' tape library, they decided on a comedy, *Annie Hall*. By nine o'clock both were hard-pressed to keep their eyes open. They were exhausted from all the energy they had expended earlier in the day. Sometime around ten o'clock, Margaret managed to awaken Reid long enough to lead him upstairs to his room, whereupon she tucked him in. Finally, Margaret collapsed into bed in the pink guest room, two doors down the hall.

True to his word, Reid awakened early the next morning and was in the process of preparing pancakes when Margaret came down the stairs and found him in the kitchen. However, at some point during his preparations, Margaret took over the project, out of respect for Julia Childs, as she put it. She managed to salvage a reasonably appetizing breakfast for both of them. Reid suggested that she stay the remainder of the day but she declined his invitation, explaining she needed to be home by mid-afternoon at the latest. So, following their leisurely breakfast and a couple of lazy hours watching the "talking heads" on the

Sunday morning news shows, they set out for Bedford at around two o'clock.

They had only been driving a few minutes when Reid glanced over at Margaret and spoke in an apologetic tone.

"Margaret, can I be so bold as to ask a very big favor of you?"

"As long as I don't have to take my clothes off or empty my wallet," came back Margaret instantaneously.

"No, nothing like that." He paused as if to summon up the courage to continue.

"As a personal favor to me, would you be willing to say that I won our little tennis match?" Shifting his eyes in her direction, he saw that she was taken aback by his request.

"It has nothing to do with some macho thing or anything like that. It's just that there are some people at the office who knew we were playing this weekend. They could really make my life miserable for the next couple of weeks if I have to go back and eat crow." Margaret did not respond but finally managed a faint smile.

"How about this, counselor? We played two sets, which we split, and then decided it was too hot to continue. How about calling it a draw?" Margaret looked over at Reid and noticed he was less than enthusiastic with the compromise.

"It's a little better, but I guarantee they'll still be all over me." Margaret sat silently, pondering his request.

"If it's that important to you, then we'll say you won. I've had a terrific time and I wouldn't want to do anything to ruin it for you," she said, placing her hand affectionately on his arm.

The conversation was guarded for the remainder of the trip back to Bedford. They agreed to report that Reid had won two-out-of-three sets played in the heat. By the time his Porsche stopped at Margaret's front door, the mood in the car had normalized. Their parting kiss extended well beyond a standard five seconds. Margaret walked to the house knowing Reid's eyes were trained on her athletic figure. Why else would he be lingering in the driveway? Unlocking the door, Margaret turned, gave him a coquettish smile, and disappeared inside the house. A quick trip upstairs found her answering machine light blinking. There had been one call. Rewinding the tape, she learned that Jenny had called and could be reached at her cabin after seven o'clock. Mother and daughter spoke for over an hour later that evening, during which Jenny was updated on the change in her mother's relationship with Brian Kelly and the specifics surrounding the new romantic interest in her life.

18

THE WEEK STARTED UNEVENTFULLY at the offices of Margaret Keogh-Olson Certified Public Accountants, except that the vacation season was now in full swing. In addition to Vern Butler, another member of the professional staff and a full-time secretary were off for the week. Added to the employees away on vacation were four more out of the office at audit sites. This resulted in an unusually quiet building. On Monday, Margaret concentrated on scheduling the professional staff for work the second half of July and on into August. The phones were very quiet, allowing her to be more productive than usual. Reid phoned at mid-morning, thanking her for what he described as one of his most enjoyable weekends in recent memory. Nothing else occurred to distinguish this Monday from any other day at the office.

Tuesday's schedule had only Margaret and Gretchen reporting to work at the Manchester building. The morning flew by and Margaret left the office at noon to jog four miles along the Merrimack River with Claire. They grabbed a salad together downtown before returning to work early in the afternoon.

Margaret's corner office on the second floor had the only private bath in the building. She took a break sometime after three o'clock, grabbing an opportunity to brush her teeth and review her appearance in the bathroom mirror. She then spent a few extra minutes in front of the mirror, something out of character for her. She was admiring her coloring from over the weekend, no doubt the result of her hours spent on the tennis court and at the pool. Stepping back into her office she stopped in her tracks. A knot of nervous energy jolted through her stomach. Brian Kelly was sitting silently in the visitor's chair directly in front of her desk. Her eyes widened as the shock of his presence continued to pass through her body.

"What are you doing here?" she blurted out. The usual warmth in Brian's eyes was not present.

"I received something in the mail and I'm returning it." Having said that, Brian produced an envelope from his pocket and sailed it over the desk in her direction. It slid across the desk's surface and fell to the floor. Reaching over to pick it up, Margaret noticed it had not been opened.

"You didn't even open my letter," she said accusingly.

"I didn't have to open it. I have a pretty good idea what it says. I've decided to bring it back to you and let you handle this matter like an adult, not a goddamn high-school kid." Brian's voice was cold.

"I want you to leave my office right now," Margaret ordered. She had recovered enough to inject some authority in the tone of her voice.

"I'm sorry, Mrs. Olson, but I drove an hour and thirty-five minutes to get here and I plan on speaking my piece before I leave," responded Brian, his voice remaining calm and low. Margaret made a motion toward the phone.

"Leave that fucking phone where it is!" he roared, causing her to let out a startled cry. She began trembling as Brian stared directly at her. This was the side of Brian she had seen many years ago in school when he faced off with Ben Turner and others.

"Believe me, I'll be leaving soon enough and you'll have the rest of your miserable life without me, but I'm taking my five minutes now." Brian's tone had softened again. Margaret suppressed the urge to cry by gritting her teeth and breathing through her nose. She knew Brian would never, under any conditions, strike her, but his anger was nonetheless unsettling.

"Now, I've given a lot of thought to this 'Dear John' letter bullshit, and I've come to the conclusion that one of two things has happened. Either your precious Brad has come slithering back to his yuppie princess—or—you have met a new Mr. Wonderful—and it's a case of out with the old and in with the new. So, which is it? I've given this a hell of a lot of thought, and it's got to be one or the other. So, which is it Mrs. Olson?"

"Can we do this at another time and another place?" asked Margaret sarcastically.

"God, you're pathetic," snarled Brian. "Right now, I wish I could be a woman for five minutes—just five minutes! I would kick your arrogant ass from one end of your hallway to the other." Brian's rage was clearly present in his words, if not his demeanor.

"Oh, that's very mature, Brian," Margaret said condescendingly.

"Oh, I'm sorry, you're right. Not returning phone calls and sending gutless letters because you don't have the nerve, or the character, to do something in person—now that's the true sign of maturity. How did I not see that?" he answered cynically.

After pausing through a moment of silence, Margaret grabbed the letter from the desk and angrily threw it at him. "It's all in the letter!" she shouted.

Brian jumped to his feet, and with the swing of his arm, sent half of the items on her desk crashing to the floor. Margaret pulled back in astonishment as a stack of client's files and a reference book were scattered across the room.

"I've met someone new, okay?" she hollered, not wanting any additional damage done to her office. A contented smile appeared on Brian's face as he stood over her desk.

"Now that makes perfect sense. In fact, it's logical. Brad would know you much better than Mr. Wonderful, hence, it would be less likely for him to return than it would be for Mr. Wonderful to enter the picture." Brian spoke mockingly, in a slow, analytical manner, as if reasoning out an argument in a philosophy class. Margaret was having difficulty responding to him, and she knew why. She knew Brian occupied all of the moral high ground on this issue. Her actions were probably indefensible. She said nothing, but continued to stare directly at him. Once again, Brian grew serious.

"There is one thing I would change if I could," he said thoughtfully. Margaret made no gesture to elicit a statement from him but Brian continued nonetheless. "Everything I said to you on my porch that rainy night—I wish I could somehow erase it. I really feel stupid—like the perfect idiot."

His voice had dropped off to a whisper. Margaret was about to pounce on his words but thought better of it and said nothing. Finally, Brian seemed to be preparing to leave. Leaning forward, his face only a few inches from her's, he resumed speaking.

"One last thing before I leave. The next time your life goes down the toilet, and if there's a God in heaven it will, don't you, under any conditions, come looking for me. Is that clear?" Brian spoke slowly in a low whisper but his words were charged with emotion. Margaret nodded yes as tears began to flow down her face. Turning to leave, an object on the edge of the desk caught his eye. He reached down and picked up the mug he had given her in the fifties room less than three months earlier. He dumped the mug's contents, pens and pencils, onto the floor.

"I think it's best if I take this back. I prefer that there be no reminders that I had ever known you. That'll keep you more focused on Mr. Wonderful," said Brian sarcastically. Then, after staring down at her silently for a moment, Brian broke eye contact and walked out of Margaret's office.

She sat motionless behind her desk, stunned by Brian's visit. She was experiencing a heavy, sinking feeling. Margaret knew she was losing a real friend. Unfortunately, Brian the friend and Brian the lover were inseparable. Slowly rising to her feet, she became aware of loud voices echoing from downstairs. Recognizing Brian's voice, Margaret quickly ran from her office and down the stairwell. Reaching the bottom, she saw Gretchen backed against the wall as Brian faced off with a policeman, whose night stick was drawn.

"Is this a fucking gag? Put the cup down?" chided Brian, facing off with the cop.

"Officer, what is going on here?" hollered Margaret as she rushed forward, stepping between Brian and the police officer.

"Ma'am, your secretary called me in to break up a disturbance. I found this individual leaving the scene."

"Officer, I'm Margaret Olson. This is my place of business. There's been a mistake. Mr. Kelly here is a businessman. We exchanged words upstairs but there has been nothing even remotely resembling a crime here," explained Margaret.

The patrolman saw in an instant that Margaret had a total grasp of the situation. He glanced over at Brian, who had, by now, relaxed his stance. The officer slipped his night stick back into its casing. Margaret sensed the patrolman was silently deliberating on how to deal with Brian's reaction to him. On the weight of Margaret's input, he reached a decision in a matter of moments.

"If you see no need for me here, I'll be on my way," he stated authoritatively. The officer turned and left the building as Margaret turned to Brian. Nothing was said as Brian walked toward the door. Turning to her with his hand on the doorknob, Brian spoke.

"Looks like I owe you one. Thank you—Margaret." Brian turned and left. Margaret felt a throbbing in the pit of her stomach as the episode abruptly ended. It was Brian's addressing her as "Margaret" that tore into her. Her proper name sounded foreboding on his lips. Gretchen approached her apologetically.

"Margaret, I'm sorry. I heard the loud voices and the sound of things hitting the floor. I heard him say something about kicking you in the hallway," exclaimed Gretchen, trying to explain her actions.

"You were put in a tough position. No harm done," assured Margaret.

"Please, no calls for me until I get back to you," she said. Returning to her office and safely behind closed doors, Margaret Keogh-Olson cried over the loss of a friend. She realized that Brian Kelly's friendship had become a luxury she could no longer afford but it tore at her nonetheless. She knew when Brian addressed her as "Margaret," it had brought certain finality to their relationship.

* * *

The month of July brought Margaret her first extended vacation in recent years. At mid-month, she and Reid left New Hampshire and sailed to Martha's Vineyard on his parents' yacht, where they planned to stay at the Birmingham summer home until early August. Vern Butler had returned from the Maritime Provinces and would run the office in Margaret's absence. The fact that Reid would devote so much of his time exclusively to her bolstered Margaret's confidence in the relationship. She was further excited by the prospect of meeting Reid's parents at the end of her stay on the island.

The logistics worked out by the Birmingham's called for the elders to drive down to Massachusetts in Reid's Porsche, then ferry across to the island. This would take place on the final weekend of Reid and Margaret's stay. In the meantime, the vacationing couple could motor around the island in the family's mint-condition, 1965 Mustang convertible. The Birmingham's kept the classic car on the island year round for such purposes. The elder Birmingham's would now have the yacht at their disposal for the remainder of the summer season. Finally, on the final day of Reid and Margaret's vacation, they would return home in his Porsche. It was to be a fabulous vacation.

* * *

In the days following the end of his relationship with Margaret, Brian withdrew into that private region where men and women retreat in the early stages of heartache. This is the period when the corridors of every personal memory are traced and retraced, when each decision and action is analyzed and questioned by the emotionally damaged survivor. After his visit to Margaret Keogh's office, Brian grew withdrawn from his associates at the complex. The chore of remaining upbeat with the general public drained every ounce of emotional energy from him. Millie watched Brian grow more and more inward as the days passed before acting on her instincts. She left Hal to handle the front desk on Friday afternoon and joined Brian on the front lawn. He had just completed the three-hour chore of cutting the four acres of plush grass that covered the property. Millie approached Brian as he crouched next to the commercial lawnmower, removing the clumps of grass wedged between the blades of the machine.

"Got a few minutes to talk to an old lady?" asked Millie in her pleasant Maine twang.

Brian lifted his head and gave his friend a forced smile. "Always got time for the girl of my dreams," he responded listlessly.

"Well, Sonny-boy, it's just that you don't seem to have been your old self these past few days, and I was thinking that if you need someone to talk things out with, well—I hope you'd come to me." Brian remained silent for a moment, as if considering a response, then nodded in the affirmative.

"Maggie broke things off last week—that's what's got me down, Millie. This has nothing to do with you or Hal and I hope neither of you read anything like that into it. It's just me dealing with a little bit of disappointment."

"I kinda figured that it was something like that when you came back to work on Tuesday. I knew you'd tell me what was going on in good time." As Brian climbed up onto the riding mower, his facial expression gave Millie the impression he was prepared to discuss his current situation.

"It's a good thing I don't get this way too often. I wouldn't have too many friends left, would I? God dammit, I've probably been happier over the last couple of months with Maggie than I've been in a long, long time. Not since Angelique, and that's been almost eight years now," he confessed.

"Don't you go an even mention that woman in the same breath as Angelique. Angel's maybe one of the most precious girls God's ever put on the planet. Don't you go and compare those two!" exploded Millie.

Brian quickly waived off Millie and continued. "Millie, it's not like I'm the sort of guy who falls in love every day. God almighty, I'm thirty-five years old and I can honestly say I've only been in love with two women in my entire life!"

Millie knew she would be wise to steer the conversation away from anything associated with Angelique LaChapelle and redirected it immediately.

"If you're interested, there's no less than a half dozen wonderful, young women at church that I can match you up with in a second. I've even had a couple ask about you recently. You just have to say the word, handsome—and it'll get done."

Brian flashed a pained expression, then looked away. "Millie, I really don't want to put myself out there at this time. First of all, it wouldn't be fair to anyone you fixed me up with. At this point I only see myself riding this whole thing out—I can only see myself holding out for the screwball notion of the real thing. You know, having the earth move under my feet—having fireworks go off when I look into the gal's eyes. I want the real thing! I don't have the energy at this time of my life to grow into loving someone. I want to have someone whose mere presence runs over me like a freight train. Angel did it— she did it big time! The only other woman I have ever met who could do this to me was Maggie, and she's done it to me twice. That's all I'm willing to settle for right now."

"Sonny-boy, you can take whatever I say with a grain of salt, but I know a little about people. I think a lot of 'Miss High and Mighty's' appeal for you goes back to the fact that she was your first love. Men are suckers for their first loves. Hell, we're all suckers for our first loves! It's just the way it is. I'd be willing to bet that if you two had come in contact for the first time back in April, you probably wouldn't have given her a second look. She just brings back certain memories and feelings from your shared past—and I'm afraid that's something you just can't change." Brian stared down on Millie for an exaggerated moment before giving her a halfhearted shrug.

"Let me give you a little more free advice, seeing that the price is right. Your uppity little Maggie May is a bit of a loose cannon if you ask me. You'd better give some thought about what you'll do if her royal highness turns around and decides to come back up here looking for you."

"That won't happen, Millie."

"And how do you know that?"

"We had quite the scene together over in Manchester. I raised my voice and threw some stuff around her office. Then, I ordered her not to try to contact me over here for any reason," Brian answered.

Millie let out a sarcastic hoot, then softened her voice.

"Listen to me, dear. Women like your lady friend don't care what you tell them—at least not at first. I'm telling you that if she changes her mind, she won't think twice about coming up here and trying to horn her way back into your life. You just better be prepared to deal with that fact should it come about. Personally, I think you're too good for the uptight, little snob. For God's sake, it's not like she was this great beauty or something."

"You don't think she's beautiful?" asked Brian in amazement.

"She's barely pretty if you ask me," sniped Millie through a chuckle. Brian climbed down from the mower while laughing out loud at Millie's assault on Margaret Keogh's appearance.

"I just don't want to see you moping around here. If it makes you feel better then I'm telling you—I don't think you've seen the last of the prissy little snob!" Brian stared down at his friend with an expression of absolute affection before enveloping Millie in a spontaneous bear hug. They walked back to the office with their arms wrapped around each other and their two spirits bonded together in mutual understanding.

19

JULY AND AUGUST HAD ALWAYS BEEN the most hectic and profitable months of the year at the Atlantic Coast Lodge. It was extremely unusual to find a vacant unit, even midweek, thanks to the marketing efforts of Brian and an impressively high rate of returning guests from year to year. The thirty-five cottages, seven motel units, and bed and breakfast operation at the main house generated about half of its annual revenue during this two-month period. Brian, Millie and Hal were more than full-time employees during this season. They were married to the complex, and often lost count of the actual number of hours they worked during the week.

For Brian, the opening of the hectic summer season of 1991 could not have come at a better time. The end of his relationship with Margaret carried with it a painful recovery period. Brian drew consolation from the calendar. He was starting his recovery period during the busy season, allowing him to immerse himself in his work. He also spent less time at the cottage by the estuary since it now harbored an abundance of bitter memories.

Brian was attending to some of the daily maintenance at the swimming pool on a weekday afternoon in late July when he noticed two young women walking down the hill in his direction. His heart sped up briefly, thinking Margaret was approaching. On closer inspection, Brian saw it was Jenny Keogh and her friend, Trudy.

"Hello, Brian," said Jenny, as the two girls reached him. He stepped back from the small shed that housed the pool's generator and lighting control panel. After applying a fatherly hug on Jenny, Brian gestured to Trudy for the same. She laughed and came forward for a weak embrace. Trudy was a studious-looking girl, with dark, bushy hair and a pleasing face set off behind a pair of fashionable granny glasses.

"So, ladies, what brings you down here, slumming from Kennebunkport?" he asked jokingly.

"Brian, we were wondering if maybe you could help us out with something, or at least find us someone who can?" asked Jenny, fumbling with her words. Brian was immediately aware of a serious overtone in her voice. He directed them to move a few steps away from the pool where they could speak privately. He gestured to Jenny to resume speaking.

"For the last two nights we haven't stayed at the cabin in Ogunquit. We've rented a motel room in Biddeford and stayed there but it's getting a little too expensive," explained Jenny.

"Whoa! Wait a minute, you're getting a little ahead of me here. Why have you been staying in Biddeford and not back at your place?" asked Brian, his eyes searching both their faces. Jenny nodded and continued.

"A couple of weeks ago I met a guy in Ogunquit and we went out a couple of times. He's got a friend who's staying in the cabin right next to ours. As I got to know him better, I saw things weren't going to work out. You know, he started talking about what he expected from the relationship." Jenny let out a long sigh. Her eyes began to fill with tears as she thought through her current situation.

"At some point I told him that I just didn't think the relationship was going anywhere—and he blew up. He's been hanging around the cabin a lot, mostly at night, and he's been making these—sort of—double-meaning comments about getting back at me. It's really starting to scare me."

"What do you mean by hanging around the cabin?" questioned Brian.

"His friend lives in the next cabin. He visits him whenever he wants and talks in a loud voice so I'll hear everything. He knows exactly what he's doing," explained Jenny, the stress of the situation now coming through in her voice.

"Dammit Jen, just move out. Find somewhere else to live," counseled Brian.

"We have, sort of, but right now all of our stuff, clothes included, is down in Ogunquit. We just don't have the money to keep staying in a motel every night. We were hoping you could give us an idea of what we could do." Jenny looked up at Brian. It was clear to him that she was in over her head and at the end of her rope. Jenny Keogh was asking him to just take care of everything for her. Whatever it was about this guy that unnerved her, Jenny needed someone else to handle it. Staring into her face, Brian was taken back by Jenny's resemblance to her mother. It sent a painful wave through him. He pushed it out of his mind.

"Have you thought of calling your mother and asking her for some help?" he questioned.

"She's away and supposedly impossible to reach," responded Jenny, hinting that her mother had been ruled out early on. Brian turned to Trudy.

"What do you think, Trudy? Is this guy as screwed up as Jenny says?"

"I won't go back there with him around. I'm afraid for both of us," Trudy confessed.

Seemingly lost in thought, Brian said nothing for a moment, then gestured to them to follow him. They strolled up the grassy hillside behind him and were led to a tiny cabin at the edge of the complex. Brian directed the two young women onto a small, screened porch, then inside a single room efficiency. The floor was stacked with corrugated boxes containing supplies of bathroom tissue, garbage bags, and other sundry items used in motels and cottages.

"If I moved these boxes back to the utility shed and turned the power back on, do you two prima donnas think you could make do with this place?" asked Brian.

The girls looked around the knotty pine cabin. In one corner was a combination refrigerator/sink with two electric burners. Beside them was a slightly worn couch, facing away from the door. Two medium-sized bureaus and a small kitchen set made up the remaining furniture in the room.

"We'd sleep on the couch?" asked Trudy.

"Not if you value your spinal cord," came back Brian, pointing toward the ceiling. Above them was a sleeping loft that extended out over the porch. Brian pulled down a ladder from the loft and when the two young women climbed the steps, they saw a full-size mattress on the floor. Pulling herself forward, Jenny crawled into the loft, pulled back a set of dusty, blue curtains, and beheld a panoramic view of Wells Harbor and the wildlife sanctuary.

"Oh God, Brian, I love it! What about you, Trudy?" asked Jenny excitedly.

"Are you kidding?" she replied, clearly impressed with the tiny unit.

"Brian, I'm not sure we can afford this on our waitressing wages and tips," declared Jenny dejectedly.

"Here's the deal, ladies. I need chambermaids desperately at this moment and I'll trade lodging for labor. I need one body every day, from nine in the morning to one in the afternoon. You work out between you—who works when. I, in return, provide the cabin, use of the pool, and other amenities at the complex. Do we have a deal?" Brian stood and watched as the two reviewed their schedules before making a commitment.

"I'm in," called out Trudy.

"Me, too," cried out Jenny, as she reached over to hug Brian.

"You get to watch the sun rise over the Atlantic right from your bed in this place," Brian attested. "The summer after my mom died I worked up here. The people who owned the cottages back then let me stay here. It's got a lot of memories for me. It's been used for a lot of things over the years, and now a couple of New Hampshire prima donnas are going to stay here. Unbelievable!" added Brian.

"There's still one more thing, Brian," said Jenny. She paused, reluctant to continue.

"We still have a lot of our clothes and stuff back at the cottage in Ogunquit. Could you have someone go down and pick it up for us? We'll pay them. I just don't want to go back and risk seeing Joe again," said Jenny timidly.

"I'll pick your stuff up," Brian said, "But I can't until tomorrow."

"I suppose we can make do with the same clothes for one more night," answered Jenny. Brian could already see the mood of the young women brighten as their anxiety eased from the prospect of making the Atlantic Coast Lodge their new, temporary home. Brian had the supply boxes removed from cottage #14 while Jenny and Trudy were at work that night.

Driving by the lodge on her way home late that evening, Jenny spotted Brian at the front desk as her Sentra crawled along the driveway. A few minutes later she joined him in the main building.

"If you're here to complain about the cottage, it's too late. It's a done deal kid," quipped Brian.

"We both know there's no way I can thank you enough for bailing us out of this mess," confessed Jenny. She fidgeted in her chair for a moment before continuing. "I know you and my mother had a falling out, and this can't be the easiest thing in the world for you." Brian smiled knowingly but did not speak. At the moment, Brian was remembering his walk with Maggie May Keogh on Parson's Beach eighteen years before, and how improbable this turn of events would have seemed to him back then.

"I had to come over and warn you about Joe Packard before anyone goes down to Ogunquit tomorrow. Joe Packard is a bastard—a mean bastard, and an awful lot of guys are afraid of him. Try to pick up our stuff when he's not there tomorrow, okay?" Jenny passed Brian a short list of things she and Trudy had left behind. He glanced down the list at the items: twelve-inch color TV, AM/FM radio, two sets of towels, small microwave, etc.

"All the crappy furniture you see goes with the place—it all stays," added Jenny. They both laughed.

"Trust me, I'll do my best to get in and out without a fuss," promised Brian, not attempting to sound macho.

"He's a big guy and he rides a motorcycle. I think that was part of what drew me to him. He was different from the boys back at school," she admitted.

"Don't feel too bad, Jen. I've always had a thing for girls on motorcycles myself," clowned Brian.

"Before I forget, how do we get phone calls from outside while we're here?" Jenny asked.

"Just tell them to call the lodge at the regular number and ask for unit fourteen. The phone's always stayed in service in case we had to reach someone working down there." Brian scribbled the phone number on a piece of paper and passed it to her. Brian stood up at the desk and the two hugged a final time before Jenny wished him a good night and headed back to her cabin.

Brian watched as she disappeared into the darkness. He was happy to help her through her present crisis but his generosity came with a price. The hectic summer season was providing him with needed distractions from the loss of Margaret Keogh, but seeing Jenny Keogh regularly, if not daily, would only aggravate an already painful recovery period. Sometime between April and June Brian had convinced himself that Margaret was the one woman who could make him happy. He now faced the prospect of having to prove himself wrong.

* * *

The following day, Brian decided upon his course of action in retrieving the girl's personal belongings from Ogunquit. It was midweek and a few units remained vacant for the day. Brian planned on taking the Ford pickup down to move Jenny and Trudy's belongings himself as soon as the NO VACANCY sign could be posted on Route 1.

Brian manned the front desk for the better part of the day. To his surprise, he was not able to fill the last vacant unit until five o'clock, putting him well behind schedule for his trip to Ogunquit. At last, with

Hal behind the front desk, Brian tossed a length of rope and a large tarp into the back of his vehicle and left.

Jenny's cabin was one of ten running parallel to Route 1, a half-mile from the village center. The cabin was situated at the very end of a complex that languished in a general state of disrepair. In their prime, the cottages had catered to vacationers visiting the region. Now it was only suitable to house seasonal workers during the prime, summer months. Brian's truck rattled down the driveway, slowly making its way to the end of a series of identical cottages. Jenny and Trudy had occupied unit #1. Brian was relieved to see little sign of human activity at this hour. Pulling up in front of the cottage, he quickly set out to complete his mission, but much to Brian's dismay, it began to rain lightly.

Nevertheless, he began by gathering up the teenagers' clothing and placing it in piles on the two beds. He had brought a few plastic bags and into these he dumped the clothing items he found on the floor and in the two bureaus. His plan was to load the clothing first, then finish up with the electronic and household articles. Beginning to realize he was running behind schedule, Brian became increasingly careless as he handled many of the items. Abruptly, there came a wave of tapping across the roof of the dingy cottage. Glancing outside, Brian saw that the rainfall had begun in earnest. Now he realized that everything would have to be covered carefully in the back of the truck.

Brian managed to slip all of the smaller clothing items, in addition to the bedding and towels, in plastic bags. After loading them onto the truck, he was about to turn his attention to the larger objects when the sound of an approaching car caught his attention. Glancing out the window, he saw an old compact car that had obviously survived many road-salt winters, pull up between the cottages. A young, slightly built fellow jumped from the vehicle and dashed into the cottage next door. Brian resumed loading the larger items, including some of the more expensive electronic equipment, as the rain began pelting down on him. Fifteen minutes later, the bulk of the work had been completed. He draped a blue tarp over the entire load and tied it down at the corners of the pickup.

Brian was hurrying through the cottage on a final pass when the roar of a motorcycle engine shook through the building. Convinced that his work was done, Brian locked the door behind him and turned toward the truck. He immediately caught sight of a man looking into the back of the vehicle, as the rain bounced audibly off the tarp. The man looked up at him.

"What the fuck do you think you're doing?" he asked in a menacing growl. From the description provided by Jenny, Brian immediately concluded that Joe Packard was speaking to him.

"A couple of gals hired me to move their stuff and I'm just finishing up," answered Brian politely. He took a moment to survey the man who had so unnerved Jenny and Trudy. Joe Packard was about Brian's height but with far more mass, weighing in at 220 or 230 pounds. He was a handsome kid, about twenty two years of age, with a full head of long hair reaching over the collar of his denim shirt. His short-sleeved shirt exposed well-developed biceps, large forearms, and huge hands. Brian was already developing a strategy in the event that a physical confrontation became necessary.

Packard walked around the truck, staring menacingly at Brian. He said nothing, but was clearly prepared for combat. Brian had already decided to see if he could lull the hulking bully into a state of over-confidence.

"Listen, I don't know what's going on, but I'm just here to earn a few bucks to put some food on the table. I'm not here to make trouble or anything," uttered Brian meekly. Brian decided that if he could avoid a physical confrontation at the price of a little personal pride, it might not be an unreasonable cost. Packard stepped forward to within Brian's personal zone.

"And where the fuck are you taking all of this shit?" he demanded. Brian walked around him and began tightening the loose ropes dangling from the tarp. A racing heartbeat now accompanied the nervous knot in his stomach.

"I've been asked to take it back to New Hampshire," declared Brian.

"I think you're full of shit! For all I know, you could be stealing everything," retorted Packard accusingly.

"Sir, if you have a problem with my removing these things, then maybe we should call the Ogunquit Police and ask for their assistance?" offered Brian. Packard erupted with laughter. Brian had now reached the conclusion that a physical confrontation was inevitable.

"Oh, I bet you'd like that, wouldn't you—shithead," snarled Packard. Brian broke eye contact with him, again hoping to lure Packard into a false sense of security.

"Maybe I should just kick your ass around the yard for a while to find out what the fuck's really going on here," bellowed the husky brute. Brian now saw Packard beginning to relax as he settled comfortably into his role of tough guy. Reaching into his back pocket as he walked toward the bully, Brian resumed speaking meekly.

"Listen, I'll give you the money I'm getting for this work, if I can just drive out of here in peace," spoke Brian timidly. Joe Packard's face gloated as Brian reached him.

"Okay fuckhead, here's—"

At that instant, Brian Kelly buried his fist into Packard's stomach just below the rib cage, driving the air back up his windpipe. Packard gasped for breath, dropping down to both knees while unable to react. Brian pounced on his helpless victim. Wrapping the fingers of his left hand around Packard's long hair, he proceeded to hammer right hand blows to Packard's right temple and to the side of his face. Following a dozen of these punches, Brian drove the unconscious biker's face into the driveway. A sickening thud accompanied the impact of Joe Packard's face on the ground. Brian was sure that the biker's nose was broken. Packard was now lying face down on the ground, motionless. Looking around, Brian noticed the fellow from the next cottage standing in the doorway.

"Move the goddamn bike out of the driveway!" Brian ordered. The young man followed his command immediately. Brian leaned back over Joe Packard, who was letting out a low moan. Grabbing him again by the hair, he lifted his head and drove it into the ground a final time. Seconds later, the motorcycle was wheeled off the driveway. Brian hoisted himself into the cab of the pickup and drove off immediately. It continued to rain.

By the time Brian arrived back in Wells, Jenny and Trudy had left for work. Pulling the truck close to the door of their cabin, Brian unloaded its contents onto the floor of the small studio. His heart continued to race from the earlier confrontation with Joe Packard. After asking Hal to continue in charge for the rest of the evening, Brian retreated to his yellow cottage down at the beach. Brian sat alone on the porch for the next hour, sipping on a can of beer he purchased back on Memorial Day. He was thinking about his confrontation with Joe Packard and how badly he could have been hurt from it, but that was not all. Brian began to ask himself if he had gone to Ogunquit for Jenny Keogh, or had he really gone for Maggie?

20

ON A SATURDAY AFTERNOON IN EARLY AUGUST, William and Elizabeth Birmingham drove onto the ferry at Woods Hole, Massachusetts, and cruised to their second home in Edgartown on the island of Martha's Vineyard. For the better part of their journey from New Hampshire the topic of conversation had been their youngest son's current female companion. Over the years they had tracked a seemingly random sequence of romantic interests with emotions ranging from amusement to grave concern. By Reid's own account, the latest woman to strike his fancy was like no one he had ever met. Margaret Olson was more serious and far more intelligent than anyone who had preceded her.

At Margaret's insistence, plans were made to dine out that evening at the Birmingham's' restaurant of choice. Margaret volunteered to pick up the tab as a token of her appreciation for the two weeks of accommodations granted her as a guest. The meticulously decorated beach house had provided a blissful setting for her and Reid. Margaret's first impression of the handsome, older couple indicated that they were withdrawn— not so much shy as uncommunicative. She hoped to draw them out of their verbal seclusion over dinner.

Reid ordered wine for the table at the outset. From there, the three Birminghams caught up on the latest social and financial developments within the family. From her spot at the quiet corner of the table, Margaret was able to learn that Reid's sister, Eve, was a corporate attorney in Philadelphia, and that William, Jr., Reid's older brother, owned and ran a small, high-tech company on the outskirts of Boston. At some point during this interlude, Margaret grew uncomfortable with the lack of attention she was receiving. She knew there was nothing she could add to the conversation, which was trapped high up in the branches of

Birmingham family tree. It was the lack of even an attempt to include her that she found troubling. Finally, Margaret welcomed the silence that came as the main course arrived and everyone went about seasoning, arranging, and carving their meals. Margaret was trying to catch Reid's eye when Mrs. Birmingham addressed her.

"Margaret, Reid tells us that you have a daughter entering college in the fall. I find that hard to believe, my dear. You look so young." Margaret responded with a smiling nod.

"No, I'm afraid it's true. My daughter Jenny enters Brown in September, but I do want you to know, Mrs. Birmingham—the flattery is not wasted on me." The slender, silver-haired woman turned to her husband.

"William, look closely at this woman," Reid's mother commented. "Does she even look thirty years old to you?" William glanced over at Margaret, then indicated she did not.

"You're making me feel like a cradle robber, mother," laughed Reid.

Margaret was beginning to become agitated. She had the distinct impression that Mrs. Birmingham was tactfully attempting to gain knowledge of her age, or perhaps it was something else. "Mrs. Birmingham, let me assure you, your son has not broken any laws by transporting me over state lines." Margaret made no attempt to disguise her sarcasm. "The truth is, I'm thirty-four. If you take a close look at me in the light, you'll see the first sign of crow's feet showing up around my eyes." Margaret gave Reid a fleeting half smile, then returned to her meal. "Well, I'm part of the conversation now!" she thought to herself.

"My dear, you must have been a child bride," came back Mrs. Birmingham, speaking in a calculated, deliberate manner. It was at that moment Margaret realized the actual reason for the interest in her age. Reid's mother had sensed the inconsistency in Margaret's appearance and the admission of a daughter into college.

"I was married at a very young age," offered Margaret, being deliberately vague.

"Mother, with Margaret in the midst of a divorce, perhaps another topic of conversation would be more appropriate," said Reid. He, too, recognized the attempt to purge Margaret of as much confidential, personal history as possible.

The exchange introduced a certain level of tension to the table. Margaret made it quite clear that she would not be pressured into any further disclosures regarding her personal affairs. Eventually, the conversation returned to small talk that dealt with the family's interests, with Margaret again excluded for the most part. Actually, for the first time in a fortnight, she began anticipating her return to New Hampshire. She thought about calling Jenny and telling her about the voyage down to the island aboard a yacht as the Birmingham's droned on about a belligerent neighbor back at Dover Point.

The Birminghams thanked Margaret for dinner as the foursome left the restaurant. Although gracious in her acceptance, Margaret limited her responses to the bare minimum. She had envisioned making a strong, first impression on the Birmingham's. Instead, she was coming away from the evening insulted, angry and hurt. Margaret had already convinced herself that Reid's family was preoccupied with some form of class distinction, and perhaps saw her as an ambitious social climber. This thought infuriated her. Arriving back at the house, Margaret excused herself almost immediately and retired for the evening.

Awaking early the next morning, Margaret changed into a running outfit before Reid had even begun to stir. Once ready for her jog, she gently shook him from his sleep and warned him not to expect her to join his family for breakfast. She explained that it was her last day on the island and she intended to take full advantage of the remaining few hours. This meant an extended run through the island's streets and foothills. Reid looked up at her, attired in black, formfitting, spandex pants and a white T-shirt. He reached out his arms, a passionate expression breaking over his face, and implored her to return to bed. Margaret turned without speaking and strode toward the door.

"I'll see you when I see you," she responded coldly without even a glance back.

At breakfast, Mrs. Birmingham expressed disappointment from the absence of Margaret at the table. In truth, she was surprised by Margaret's boldly independent gesture and saw it for what it was— retribution for the night before. Three hours later, the Birminghams were all seated in wicker chairs on the front porch when Margaret finally returned. She stepped onto the porch, looking magnificently fit in her running togs. Even the chronically predisposed William Birmingham lifted his eyes from his *Sunday New York Times* and took in, at length, the physical specimen that was Margaret Keogh-Olson.

Margaret offered her hosts an offhanded apology for missing breakfast. In almost the next breath, she asked Reid when he planned to leave for the mainland. While not being overtly rude, she was letting everyone know she was ready to leave. Reid advised her that he hoped to leave at noon. The word on their exact schedule provided Margaret with an excuse to return to their bedroom to pack.

* * *

Margaret and Reid arrived on the mainland that afternoon following a polite, albeit not warm, send-off by the elder Birminghams. Aboard the ferry, the conversation between Margaret and Reid was stunted, but not unpleasant. Both agreed it would be good to see New Hampshire again as Reid's Porsche pulled away from the ferry terminal. Shortly after, Margaret asked Reid if he would turn into a convenience store before they joined the highway in a few miles. Less than a mile later, Reid rolled into the parking lot of a twenty-four-hour superette. Margaret jumped from the car and hurried inside. Reappearing a few minutes later, she carried a supersized soft drink and two cheese Danish. The passenger window of the Porsche came down as she reached the car.

"I hope you're not thinking of bringing that into the car?" he asked accusingly.

"Yes, I am," she shot back defiantly.

"Jesus, this is a sixty-thousand-dollar car!" he cried out.

"I'm sorry Reid, but I'm hungry! I'll be very careful," she said apologetically.

"I really wish you wouldn't," he answered, making no effort to assist her with the door.

Margaret stared at him for a moment, allowing anger to show through on her face. "Fine—then kindly remove my luggage from the car and I'll take care of getting myself home," she called out.

Reid let out an agitated sigh but was not ready to concede. "I'm not unloading your luggage," he stated with resolve.

"Then kindly drop it off at the house in Bedford when you get back. Put it out back where no one can see it from the road," she instructed. Margaret turned and walked to a public telephone on the side of the store. Putting her junk food down on the ground beside her, she began fumbling through the yellow pages of the telephone book beneath the phone. Seconds later, Reid called out to her to get back into the car. Reaching the Porsche, she stood motionless at the passenger door until Reid jumped from behind the wheel and opened, then closed, the door for her. Margaret carefully tore open the wrapper from her Danish and took a bite as Reid reentered the car. Margaret was wearing her cocky smile. She had called his bluff and Reid had blinked first.

"You should have eaten back at the house," he barked.

"No, I think I'd pretty much had my fill of the Birmingham family update from the night before," she explained coldly.

"You can't take what my parents say so personally. It's a generation thing," he explained.

"That's horseshit and you know it. Your mother wanted to know everything about me and my daughter—and it's none of her goddamn business—period! The truth is, you should have said something last night when your mother started probing, and you didn't!"

The Porsche was still idling in the corner of the parking lot. The handsome attorney was not finished. "One last thing, Margaret. Why does every disagreement or argument between us have to be resolved with an entry to your 'win' column? Would you tell me that?"

Margaret paused before answering him. "That's because I don't even allow myself the luxury of a 'loss' column."

Reid did not respond to her statement. Glancing first into the rear view mirror, he pulled the car back onto the road and resumed the trip home. He was angry at her but was nonetheless impressed with her resolve. He decided to let the argument die at this point. Margaret Olson was like no other woman he had ever encountered. This was part of what drew him to her. Following fifteen minutes of unbroken silence, Margaret offered Reid a sip of her soda in her best Shirley Temple voice. Strangely, it struck a chord and he laughed, practically against his will. The two lovers mended fences over the remainder of the trip to New Hampshire.

After unloading Margaret's luggage and assorted other belongings from the car, they shared a long, good-bye kiss and Reid headed back home to Manchester. Margaret was suddenly overjoyed to be home and under her own roof. Despite the last few hours on the island, the sailing, the Gulf Stream water of Martha's Vineyard, the leisurely pace of the last two weeks, it had all been great. However, now it was comforting to be home. Leaving the luggage and loose clothing in a heap downstairs, she walked upstairs to her office and counted the blinks on her answering machine—fifteen. She sat down, rewound the tape while hunting for a pencil and paper, and hit the play button. About midway through the messages she heard Jenny's voice:

"Hello mother, I figured I'd get the machine. Just calling to let you know that we've had to move. Trudy and I are up in Wells now. We're staying in a cabin at the Atlantic Coast Lodge, unit # 14. So, if you need to get in touch you can reach me through their switchboard or at Dunbar's, of course. If not, I'll call you early next week. Love you!"

Margaret stopped the machine. She began to boil as she started to theorize how Brian had gotten the girls to relocate up in Wells with him. It was after five o'clock so Margaret called Jenny's number at the restaurant, but she got a busy signal. Margaret skipped downstairs to the kitchen and pulled a bottle of mineral water from the refrigerator. She had a suspicion that Brian Kelly was up to something. Redialing Jenny's number at work, she found it was still busy. Setting her phone index to the letter "A," she found the number for the Atlantic Coast Lodge and dialed. After a single ring a male voice answered, but it was not Brian.

"Brian Kelly, please," Margaret demanded. There was a momentary shuffle.

"Brian Kelly, can I help you?" he said courteously.

"I just got home and received a message on my voice mail from my daughter. She said she could no longer be reached in Ogunquit, and that she was now living up in Wells at your complex. Brian, what the hell is going on up there?" asked Margaret accusingly.

"Have you spoken to Jenny yet?" inquired Brian calmly.

"I can't get through on the line to the restaurant," came back Margaret.

"I think it'd be best if she told you herself." Brian remained speaking slowly and calmly.

"If this is part of some moronic scheme to get back at me through my daughter, then let me warn you...."

"Mrs. Olson, you're making an idiot of yourself here. Wait and talk to Jenny before you begin shooting off your mouth," advised Brian calmly.

"Why can't you tell me?" continued Margaret.

"It's not my place to tell you, it's hers. There may be things she doesn't want you to know," he reasoned.

"And this is not some stupid way to get back at me?" questioned Margaret, her voice beginning to soften.

"Speak to Jenny about it. I'm sure then, it'll all make sense. If you want, I'll leave a message on her door and have her call you tonight when she gets in."

"Yes, I'd really appreciate that." Margaret paused for a few, uncomfortable moments and then continued.

"And how are things going for you?" she asked. Brian knew the question was about his mental state.

"You don't have to worry, Mrs. Olson—I'll live."

"And Jenny is perfectly okay?" she queried.

"Never been better as far as I can tell," responded Brian in an uncharacteristically subdued manner. That instant, another line could be heard ringing at his desk and he thankfully used it to bring the conversation to a close. Reassuring Margaret that Jenny would get her message, Brian politely wished her a pleasant day before answering the other call. Margaret hung up the phone, relieved her daughter was in no trouble. Although tired from the day's activities, she decided to wait up for Jenny's call.

Later in the evening, as she sat alone in the living room with only classical music to mask the silence in the house, Margaret thought of Brian. It had been good to hear his voice, although his quiet, distant manner had been discomforting. She took some consolation from the fact that he had spoken to her, and not just dismissed her call. As she sat alone in the quiet house, Margaret became acutely aware that she missed her friend.

At eleven thirty Margaret was awakened by the phone. Running to the kitchen, she picked up the receiver and heard her daughter's voice. Over the next forty-five minutes, mother and daughter updated each other on the details of their lives since they had last spoken. Jenny explained the circumstances that drove her and Trudy to deposit themselves helplessly on Brian Kelly's doorstep. Her mother assured Jenny that she had done the right thing.

21

THE FOLLOWING MORNING, just moments after arriving at the office, Margaret jotted down a short note and sealed it inside a blank envelope.

> Brian,
>
> *As you predicted, I did feel a little foolish after speaking to Jenny. This short note is to say I'm sorry and to thank you for helping Jen out.*
>
> Margaret

With the note safely sealed inside an envelope, Margaret asked one of her senior auditors to address it for her and mail it later in the day from Portsmouth. The auditor was scheduled to begin field work in that seacoast city on an engagement. She wanted the envelope to arrive at the Atlantic Coast Lodge bearing an unfamiliar handwriting and a Portsmouth postmark. Margaret felt this maneuver guaranteed that Brian would not suspect the note was from her and not return it unopened as he had the last one.

Margaret's weekly schedule had begun to develop a pattern. She would schedule lunch with Reid on Tuesdays and have Claire as an overnight guest on Wednesdays. Weekends found her joining Reid for dinner, a movie, live theater, or occasionally dancing. However, on the weekend following her return from Martha's Vineyard, Margaret planned to join Jenny up in Maine.

On Wednesday night, with Claire sitting contentedly on the couch clutching a glass of California white wine, Margaret punched out the number of the Atlantic Coast Lodge. She hoped to reach Jenny on her daughter's only night off. After a single ring, a woman answered the telephone.

"Atlantic Coast Lodge, can I help you?"

"Millie, it's Margaret Olson calling for my daughter. Do you know if Jenny's in?" she asked politely.

"I'll put you through," responded Millie, with not a word of recognition for Margaret. The phone rang three times.

"Hello." It was Jenny.

"Jenny, it's your mother calling to check up on you."

Jenny responded with a long sigh. "You caught me in the loft. That's why I sound so out of breath—from scurrying down the ladder."

"I'm still trying to picture which of those cottages Brian has dumped you in," moaned Margaret.

"I told you, Mother, it's sort of in the corner of the complex, by the edge of the motel building. Hell, it's almost big enough for Trudy and I to stand in side by side at the same time," joked Jenny.

"Well, daughter dear, I was calling to see how you and Trudy would feel about putting your mother up for the weekend? It's not like I've spent much time with my favorite daughter lately."

"You mean stay here?" questioned Jenny.

"Jenny, it can't be that small! There has to be a couch or something I can sleep on?" insisted Margaret.

"What about Brian?" Jenny asked, almost in disbelief.

"We spoke on Sunday. Brian seemed okay," replied Margaret.

"Mother, he's not okay. I really don't think it's such a good idea— you coming here, I mean. What about coming up on Friday night and getting a place over in Kennebunkport? I'll stay with you there." Jenny waited for her mother's response.

"If you think that's best then that's what I'll do. The important thing is that I spend some quality time with you, stranger." The conversation shifted to planning an itinerary for the two. This meant working around Jenny's schedule at the restaurant and the lodge.

As Margaret wrapped up her long conversation with Jenny, she promised to make reservations for the weekend somewhere in the Kennebunkport area. During this interlude, Claire had sat cross-legged on the couch sipping on her glass of wine. By the time Margaret focused her attention back on her friend, Claire's face showed evidence of a slight buzz from the California white. Claire rose and, stepping over her shoes, refilled both their glasses. Margaret sensed that her friend desperately wanted to talk.

"I've been thinking about doing something but I wanted to run it by you first," confessed Claire.

"Sure, go ahead, kid. God knows I run enough things by you."

"Well, you see, it involves Brian," uttered Claire sheepishly. Margaret's eyes widened with interest.

"I've—I've been thinking about calling him to see if he'd like some company. You know, a movie or dinner—something innocent." Claire stared at Margaret, who appeared shocked.

"Why Brian?" Margaret blurted out.

"Why not Brian? We got along great at Jenny's graduation party and you've told me so much about him, I feel like I already know him. Margaret, so help me, if this is a problem, well, this is why I'm asking you. I don't want to cause a rift between us," explained Claire, reflecting the delicacy of the situation.

"Do you find him attractive?" questioned Margaret, still taken aback by her friend's statement.

"Yes, he's a good-looking guy, not Reid Birmingham good looking, sort of an everyday good looking," Claire continued, seeing Margaret was still speechless. "Part of it has to do with the way you two were before you met Reid. You'd come home from Wells and talk about his romantic little house—and all the attention he paid you—and how you'd go for these long walks on the beach. You made me so goddamn jealous! I think I need something like that in my life right now," confessed Claire.

"Did I talk about the sex, too?" blurted out Margaret.

"Of course!" exclaimed Claire. They both burst out laughing.

"Margaret, you can't believe the collection of clowns I've been out with over the last six months," confided Claire, her mood growing melancholy. "But for all I know, Brian might not even want to go out with me," lamented Claire.

"Yeah, sure," said Margaret, replied. "All I have to do is think about the look he had on his face with you on his lap that night at the party. He looked a little too happy." Margaret suddenly felt jealous, especially when her comment seemed to cheer Claire for a moment. She got up from her chair and joined Claire on the couch.

"Let me share something with you, Claire. Over the past few days I've been thinking of Brian a lot myself. I still know I did the right thing when I broke things off. There was no way I was going to find time to see if Reid was the type of man I really wanted with Brian in the way. Anyway, all of a sudden I've started thinking about whether he's seeing someone else, and maybe getting involved." A disapproving look came over Claire's face.

"I know, I know, who the hell am I to feel this way? It's like I don't want him but I don't want anyone else to have him. Suddenly, I have this proprietary feeling about Brian. I spoke to him, very briefly the other night when I called for Jenny, and that seems to have triggered this mild depression I'm going through."

"You haven't said a word about your vacation with Reid," observed Claire.

"Claire, the trip down to the island on the yacht was beyond belief. At first I was a little scared, not knowing how knowledgeable Reid was at sailing, but once I was sure he knew what he was doing it was magnificent!" Margaret caught herself drifting off from the subject at hand. Stretching out her arm, she applied an affectionate hug around Claire's shoulder.

"How about this. You give me a couple of weeks to get this craziness about Brian Kelly's love life out of my system and then, we'll send him another New Hampshire femme fatale. God help him!" wisecracked Margaret.

22

BECAUSE SHE finished packing for her weekend with Jenny on Thursday night, Margaret was able to leave directly from work the next day. She had reserved a motel room on Route 9 in Kennebunk. It was mid-August and the traffic in and around the beach communities on Friday night was dreadful. Margaret managed to reach the motel by seven. After tossing her luggage and supplies on the beds, she headed into Kennebunkport to dine at Dunbar's. Margaret was forced to wait thirty minutes to be seated. She killed time seated at a small table in the bar where she politely rejected the advances of two gentlemen, including one who appeared underage. Finally, Margaret was beckoned upstairs and seated at a table by a window in Jenny's section. The weekend started on the right note as Margaret socialized with her daughter who had spent the summer honing her hospitality skills.

Jenny had loaned Trudy her car for the weekend to minimize the inconvenience of getting to work and back caused by her mother's visit. Margaret picked up Jenny at closing time and the two drove back to the motel. She shared the story of the young man in the bar, prompting Jenny to offer her own account of advances from male tourists, many old enough to be her father. It was a warm, humid night and the mother and daughter ventured out to a nearby ice cream stand, managing to order a couple of black-and-white frappes just as the lights in the place were going out. Margaret took the long route back to the motel allowing the two women to catch up on each other's lives. The air was still warm and humid as they climbed out of the BMW and entered the motel.

Jenny was in the process of placing a few of her clothes on hangers when she offhandedly tossed a question to her mother. "How serious is this thing with Reid Birmingham?"

Her mother was caught by surprise. "That's really hard to say, honey. Why do you ask?"

"You're my mother. I wonder about things like that, that's all."

"By any chance, did someone ask you to ask me that?" she asked.

"If you mean Brian—no! Mother, he doesn't even mention your name. Even if I forget and bring you up, he doesn't say a thing and quickly changes the subject."

"You know, we spoke briefly on Sunday. I wound up sending him an apology card the next day," confessed Margaret.

"That must be what he and Millie were talking about the other day. I walked in on Millie the other morning going on about something Brian got in the mail. They sort of shut right up as soon as they saw me," added Jenny.

"I don't think I'm one of Millie's favorite people based on the cold shoulder I got the other night when I called you."

"Millie and Brian are very close. You really can't blame her for being that way," Jenny replied. Margaret crossed the room and hugged her daughter.

"I miss you," she confessed.

"I love and miss you, too," responded Jenny while slipping under the covers in her bed. The air conditioner managed to turn the room cool enough for a light blanket. There was not a sound for the next few minutes except the whirring of the air conditioner and the noise from an occasional car on Route 9. Then, Margaret heard Jenny roll over onto her side.

"Are you in love with Reid?" she asked in a low voice.

"I honestly don't know," responded her mother.

* * *

Saturday morning, mother and daughter showered, dressed, and were on the road by nine o'clock. After stopping in Kennebunk Village for breakfast they headed north for a day of shopping in the Old Port section of Portland. Under instructions from her mother, Jenny took this opportunity to add to her wardrobe for Brown University. Margaret would not allow Jenny to pay for anything, advising her to bring the savings from her summer work to Rhode Island with her.

Margaret felt her spirits lift from the time spent with her daughter, convincing her that the idea of spending the weekend in Maine with Jenny had been a good one. At her daughter's request, they grabbed lunch at a sidewalk café before resuming their shopping blitz in the early afternoon. Unfortunately, Margaret's mood dampened later on when Jenny reminded her that they must return to Kennebunkport for her four o'clock shift. While dropping her daughter off, Margaret made a 6:30 reservation for herself. Following her return to the motel, Margaret changed into a running outfit and set out for Parson's Beach.

In a matter of seconds, Margaret was legging her way along the road leading to the beach. The motel was only a hundred yards or so from the roadway to the beach, a fact she had not realized when the reservation was made. The run gave her time to internalize the small role this remote beach had played in her life. She thought again of the trips made here with Brian Kelly during her pregnancy. Margaret soon found herself thinking on a different plane as she jogged up the road. Running sometime did this to her. She considered how odd it was that Brian Kelly was around when Jenny entered her life, and now, eighteen years later, he was again present as Jenny prepared to leave home for college and exit her mother's life. Margaret marveled at how improbable these events seemed.

Jogging over the small bridge leading into the parking area, she observed the tidewater rushing out to the open ocean on the far side of the dunes. There were still a dozen or so people loitering in the area, all couples. Reaching the edge of the ocean, she decided to head south. Margaret usually used her jogging time to sort out business, financial and personal affairs but only personal matters came to mind on this afternoon.

Parson's Beach ran for a half-mile in this direction before a rocky point interrupted the sandy expanse. Margaret continued to mull over a number of situations as she jogged along. She recalled her conversation with Claire on Wednesday night. In a couple of weeks Claire might be contacting Brian, and who could predict where that might lead? It struck Margaret that she was still thinking of him as her fallback guy, even after the scene in the office. Brian had told her not to contact him under any conditions, but nonetheless, Margaret felt that she still maintained some level of influence over him. She knew that might change with Claire in the picture. These things tumbled in her mind as she strode alongside the foaming surf.

Then, unexpectedly, she spotted a familiar object thirty feet ahead. She abruptly pulled up, walked over and stared at the odd-shaped rock she and Brian had sat on eighteen summers earlier. In April they had searched in vain for it, and now here it was prominently exposed above the beach sand. Momentarily puzzled, she quickly deduced that the shifting sand caused by the action of the tide must have covered it in the spring. After removing a few strands of seaweed, she sat down and looked out over the Atlantic. The coastline seemed more sober and moody than she remembered. In the past, Brian always had been beside her on this spot. The rays of the sun were casting shadows over her shoulder. Remembering the note she mailed Brian on Monday, Margaret considered the fact that he had not responded. She had expected a call, or perhaps a cryptic note in return.

Removing her sneakers, Margaret poured out the sand that had collected during the beach leg of her run. She was growing melancholy again. It was as if she had broken herself away from her recurring gloom by running along the coast. However, the gloom had taken advantage of Margaret's meditative stop by closing the distance between it and her. Now, she felt it reattach itself to her. This place lent itself to both fond and bitter memories. Following twenty minutes of meditation, Margaret jogged back to the motel, sprinting the last four-hundred yards.

Margaret started back for New Hampshire shortly after noon on Sunday. She fell prey to an uncharacteristic display of emotion while exchanging good-byes with Jenny as they parted at Dunbar's back door. She apologized to her daughter, who in turn promised to visit home before relocating to the Brown campus in early September. Deciding to forego the highway, she traveled south on Route 1 and passed the entrance to the Atlantic Coast Lodge. Involuntarily glancing up the driveway, Margaret only managed to catch a fleeting glimpse of Brian's Ford pickup parked in front of the storage shed. Ninety minutes later, the BMW pulled into her driveway in Bedford.

Margaret pushed open her front door with the key still secured in the lock and felt the stillness and quiet trapped inside rush up and envelope her. It was as if she could literally feel herself breaking the absence of a human presence within the building. Walking down the hall and into the kitchen she became profoundly aware that only her actions were interrupting the deep silence that regularly pervade her home. After picking at a plate of old leftovers from the fridge and catching the evening news she retreated to her home office upstairs and put in two hours of work. It was barely nine o'clock when she turned off her computer and began staring at the blank monitor. Margaret caught herself replaying Brad's speech the night he had walked out of her life. It had been in this very room. A few moments later Margaret was weeping aloud, uncontrollably.

Opening the office the next morning, Margaret plunged herself into her "to do" list immediately. Reid made his customary Monday morning call before nine, confirming lunch on Tuesday and asking her to accompany him to a going-away party for Ned Seavey, a business associate. Margaret agreed, and after providing the obligatory details of her weekend in Maine, returned to her workload. She worked out the remainder of her weekly social calendar later in the morning. Margaret reserved a tennis court on Wednesday night for her and Claire, then called her mom and asked if a Thursday visit home would cause a problem. Her question was greeted by an invitation to supper that night from her parents.

23

MARGARET ARRIVED AT THE TENNIS CLUB Wednesday night behind schedule, leaving her only a few minutes to change before taking to the court. Although on the court by six, Margaret and Claire could not finish two sets before their hour elapsed. The first set had been unusually competitive with Margaret finally prevailing, 7-5. The second set was knotted at three apiece when the hour ran out. Claire laughingly chided Margaret for not keeping her mind on her game as the two packed their gear and prepared to exit for the dressing room. Turning to leave, a short fellow approached the two women.

"Margaret Olson, right?" he asked, extending his hand. Margaret nodded yes and promptly introduced Claire.

"Harry Shapiro—I work with Reid and you've been pointed out to me here at the club. I had to come over and tell you you're a hell of a tennis player, and I can't believe Reid actually beat you a few weeks ago." Margaret smiled, giving a halfhearted shrug of the shoulders.

"You know, you cost me twenty bucks, but if there's ever a rematch, I'd bet on you again," he said with a guffaw.

"You lost twenty dollars betting on me?" Margaret asked.

"No big deal, Ned Seavey had to cough up a hundred!"

"I hope that's not why he's leaving?" quipped Claire in a wink of an eye.

"God, if I'd known there was so much money riding on me, I might have played harder," exclaimed Margaret as she tried to mask her concern. A voice cried out from across the club and the jovial attorney excused himself from the conversation.

Margaret and Claire picked up Chinese food en route to Bedford, throwing all of their health and dietary concerns to the wind. During dinner they playfully lamented the harm that sweet and sour chicken, beef teriyaki, and pork fried rice was doing to their bodies. Margaret broke out twin bottles of wine to wash down the sinfully unhealthy dinner.

"Oh, Margaret, before I forget. I've sort of ruled out that idea I had about calling Brian Kelly and maybe starting something up. I started thinking about it and—Jesus, I have a problem keeping a relationship going with someone in Nashua! How would that thing ever work?" asked Claire rhetorically. Margaret looked across the table and acknowledged her friend's statement but did not speak.

"Are you okay?" asked Claire, worried by her friend's silence. Margaret shrugged her shoulders.

"I'm really not very happy, if that's what you mean," Margaret answered dispiritedly. For some reason, Margaret's admission struck a nerve. Claire exploded on the spot.

"God-dammit—you have it all! What's the hell's the matter with you? You have this successful CPA firm where everyone has to answer to you—boss lady! You have this wonderful house, which is yours, all yours! You're a terrific-looking woman and you seem to be able to get any man you want right now! What the fuck more do you want? Jesus, Margaret, wake up!" shouted Claire. At the moment, Claire was frustrated by her friend and the wine was stripping her of any inhibitions.

"What would you do if you were me?" asked Margaret, almost pathetically.

"About what?" questioned Claire.

"I think you have a pretty good idea of what I'm talking about—about why I'm miserable. What would you do, Claire?"

"You can't ask me to make that kind of a decision for you."

"If I turn my back on Reid, I will be second guessing myself for the rest of my life. There are people who have success stamped all over them. Reid's one of them," stated Margaret authoritatively.

"I think his old man's bucks have a little to do with that, don't you?" retorted Claire sarcastically.

"You said yourself—he'll probably be governor some day. How could I live with the knowledge that I walked away from someone like that—for Brian?"

"Jesus, Margaret, you talk about Brian like he lived on the street. He isn't exactly some no account. You told me he owns a piece of that business he runs and he does own his own home," declared Claire impatiently. Margaret reached down for her wine, lost in thought. A tender look came over Margaret's face followed by a smile.

"Calling Brian's place a home is a bit of a stretch," chuckled Margaret. Margaret's face turned serious again as she resumed speaking.

"Can you keep a secret?" she asked.

"Not if you can't," Claire joked.

"That tennis match with Reid—our first date tennis match. Well, I won, not him. I just agreed to say I lost because he was afraid of the ribbing he might get."

Claire's mouth dropped open. "This is the match your chubby friend at the club lost twenty bucks on?" quizzed Claire.

Margaret nodded yes.

"You certainly don't think that Reid asked you to cover for him for the money, do you?" asked an astonished Claire.

"I don't know. It's just one more thing that troubles me about Reid. Three weeks ago I would have followed him to the end of the earth and today I'm sitting here second-guessing myself. In the end though—I know I'll stay with Reid, that's a given."

"And how do you know—for sure, I mean?" Claire asked.

"My heart doesn't have the same influence as my head. In the end, my head will make the decision. I've always been that way," insisted Margaret. She took another sip of her wine. A thoughtful look covered her face as she turned something over in her mind.

"It's funny, Brian and I had a discussion about something along these lines a couple of months ago. He was telling me about this guy he knew who did all these crazy things because of a woman—I can't remember what. Anyway, Brian finished up his story by quoting some French philosopher—'The mind is always the dupe of the heart'—that was the quote. Naturally, I disagreed and told him my decisions came from my head, but he just kept repeating—'The mind is always the dupe of the heart.' Claire, Brian is so strange." Claire laughed.

"Strange, in a nice way," added Margaret, her mind seemingly off somewhere else.

Jenny called later in the evening. Margaret was thrilled to learn that her daughter had given her notice at Dunbar's and told Brian that Sunday, August 25th, would be her last day. Jenny was coming home and would spend more than a week at the house. Trudy had also given her notice, but she was staying on at the cabin and working for Brian full-time before heading off to college. The news lifted Margaret's spirits for the remainder of the evening.

* * *

On Thursday night Mrs. Keogh served meat loaf, one of Margaret's favorite meals when she was growing up. Margaret had looked forward all day to joining her parents for dinner. A nostalgic wave swept over her as she helped her mom set the table while her dad sat reading the *Manchester Union Leader* in the den. The conversation was light and unforced during the meal as the Keogh family reminisced over humorous incidents that occurred during Margaret's childhood. Following dessert, as was his custom, Mr. Keogh returned to the den and resumed reading his paper. Keeping with the nostalgic theme of the evening, Margaret joined her mother at the sink, assisting her with the dishes. She could not resist chiding her mom for the hundredth time or so for not investing in a dishwasher. Mrs. Keogh wore a contented look on her face as she ignored her daughter's teasing and continued washing.

"I really find it amazing that Jenny would spend the summer at Brian Kelly's motel, of all places. It is such a small world," observed the silver-haired woman. Her mother's observation had come from nowhere, clueing Margaret that something else was on her mind.

"Now, the fellow you're seeing—where is he from?" asked Mrs. Keogh. Margaret knew immediately that she was expected to provide some background information on Reid Birmingham.

"He's from Dover, Mother."

"And how did you two meet?"

"He was the first lawyer I spoke to about the divorce. We began seeing each other a short time later. His family is quite wealthy," added Margaret, prompting only a meager acknowledgment from her mother.

"It's funny dear, but when I saw the way you and Brian were carrying on at Jenny's graduation party, I told your father on the way home that it wouldn't be long before you'd be making an announcement." Mrs. Keogh looked up at her daughter. It was her way of cueing her for an explanation, but Margaret only gave off a shrug. She was sure her mother would never understand. After completing the dishes, Margaret watched a little TV with her parents before heading home. However, she had thoroughly enjoyed her time back at the old house with her folks.

It was only ten o'clock when Margaret cruised up the driveway to her house. Foregoing use of the garage, she pushed open the front door, set the alarm system and bounded upstairs to her office. The drive home had proven productive. An idea for potential cost savings on the practice's travel, meals and entertainment had cropped up between her parent's house and home. Margaret wasted no time. Sitting at her desk, she pecked out a memo to her secretary outlining a project in this area.

As Margaret waited on the printer to spit out three hard copies of the memo, she caught herself gazing at the black, leather chair against the near wall. It was the chair Brad had sat in the night he delivered his painful resignation from their marriage. Margaret thought back on that disturbing evening and was struck by how recent an event it was. Brad Olson had been her lifemate, her bedmate, her other half, only eight short months before. This fact struck her as so astonishing, she literally had to rethink 1991 to assure herself she had not misplaced a year somewhere in her memory.

A pang of bitterness swept over her. Margaret knew that, in all likelihood, Brad was happy in his new life. She had picked up on this during their luncheon meeting a few months ago. There was something about this circumstance that she found terribly unsettling. An overwhelming desire to speak to someone about these feelings was coming over her. She had used Claire as a sounding board only twenty-four hours earlier and therefore quickly ruled her out. Reid, on the other hand, had always seemed preoccupied whenever Margaret managed to steer a conversation in such a direction. A glance at the office clock told her the front desk at the Atlantic Coast Lodge was still open. She reasoned there was a high probability that Brian would be working the desk until closing. Margaret decided to call the lodge, presumably in an attempt to reach Jenny. Once on the phone, she would ease her way into a conversation with Brian, something light and innocent. It would be good to speak with her old friend and perhaps take a first step toward normalizing their relationship, she thought. Margaret's stomach tightened in anticipation as she punched the buttons on the phone.

"Atlantic Coast Lodge, this is Millie speaking, can I help you?" asked a familiar voice seventy miles away. Margaret's spirits plummeted at the sound of Millie's voice and she hung up without speaking a word. The quiet, empty house seem to magnify the sound of her footsteps as she left her office after shutting off her computer and proceeded down the hallway to her bedroom. While preparing for bed she concluded that the aborted phone call to Maine was ill-advised if not downright foolish.

Margaret set her alarm for five o'clock Friday morning to ensure an early arrival at the office. She would be cutting out of the office early to join Reid later in the day, but first she wanted to squeeze in at least eight hours of work. On the drive into the city she thought over some of the details from dinner with her parents the night before. The evening had been quite enjoyable and Margaret questioned why she had not thought of inviting herself over before. The dreary mood that had been her companion over the past couple of weeks was back and a persistent, nervous pressure was now present in her stomach. Margaret made up her mind to run an extra couple of miles at noon to give herself a little relief from this condition.

Reid called late in the morning and arranged to meet Margaret at the Executive Tower Café at four-thirty. He expected a minimum of three dozen professionals to show up for Ned Seavey's going-away party. Margaret made a mental note to replenish her supply of business cards. Tonight could prove to be a prime networking opportunity, she thought. She was also delighted to learn that Claire would be there, providing her with some female companionship.

Margaret and Reid met in the parking lot of the Executive Tower as planned. After riding together in the elevator to the tenth floor, they found a handful of his associates already standing around and chatting. All appeared to be lawyer types, complete with button-down shirts, wide suspenders, and wing tips. The law office had reserved a function room at the far end of the floor. The rest of the establishment consisted of an open floor covered by circular dining tables and a small stage. Though it was her custom to politely introduce herself in similar situations as this, this afternoon she lacked the desire. Instead, she was content to stand quietly at the edge of a group of professionals, merely nodding her head at appropriate times. Following his return with their beverages, Reid got caught up in the conversation, spoken mostly in legalese.

At one point Margaret turned at the sound of the elevator's doors opening. Stepping out was Claire, accompanied by an elderly attorney. She had met the managing partner of Eggleston, Sanders & Cohen at the elevator door below and was happy to have an escort for her arrival. Dashing over to the two, Margaret made haste to announce that she would not allow her friend to monopolize the time of the best-looking man in the room. The three laughed, then for the next few minutes Margaret and Claire politely allowed the refined Mr. Eggleston to shower them with compliments.

Eventually, Ned Seavey made his entrance to a chorus of well-wishes and humorous warnings about what to expect down in Boston. By now the function room was open to the attendees and no less than forty men and women crowded between its walls. Margaret learned from Reid that after their meal there would be a roast, at which time a few of his associates would attempt to humiliate Attorney Seavey with fact and fiction.

Margaret was seated next to Reid at the far end of the table, some distance from Claire. She remained intently quiet, taking in everything around her. Margaret learned of the latest business casualties from the recession, and who might be next. She overheard whispers about who screwed up at the office, and at what cost. By pretending to be listening to a totally different conversation, Margaret gained knowledge of the identity of a paraprofessional at Reid's office who could be compromised, followed by a lesson plan on how. This was a game, Margaret's game, but on this day she was seeing it for what it was—small and petty. Glancing over at Reid, she saw that he was caught up in a conversation across the table. Inexplicably, she began thinking of her time in the canoe on the estuary in Wells. That told her she needed to get away from the table.

"Pardon me, Reid, I have to visit the ladies room," she said while pulling out her chair. He smiled at her and nodded.

Margaret left the gathering through a door directly behind her, then glanced around the large main room for the lavatories. She soon spotted them some distance away over by the double doors leading out to the kitchen. Negotiating the narrow walking corridor between tables, trays, waiters, and milling customers, Margaret was only a few steps from the ladies room when a busboy transporting an overloaded tray of dirty dishes struck her arm. The impact from the accidental bump threw his load off balance, sending the tray and its contents crashing to the floor. Cries from startled customers instantaneously rose from the gathering, causing Margaret to freeze in her tracks. Dropping to his knees, the busboy scurried to pick up the glassware and china, hurriedly piling them back onto the tray. Someone hollered from inside the kitchen. Margaret, still a little shocked, looked down at the young man at her feet.

"I'm—sorry—ma'am," sounded a deliberate voice. A look of tremendous anxiety covered the broad face of this young busboy who clearly labored under the affliction of Down's syndrome. His hands shook as he attempted to stack the remaining items back on the tray.

"I am so very sorry for this," came a voice approaching from across the room. A well-dressed, middle-aged man, clearly the owner or manager, walked up to Margaret. She still had not spoken.

"This is a mistake, a terrible mistake," said the manager as he stared disdainfully down on the young man. "They come by here and pressure us into giving jobs to these people. They're not the ones who deal with the consequences," he growled. Margaret remained frozen in her tracks. Her mind flashed back to the forlorn waitress at Perkin's Cove and the embarrassment she had felt dropping her tray. Margaret thought of Brian Kelly. She had no doubt what Brian would do under these same circumstances.

"No sir, you're mistaken. I'm afraid this is clearly my fault. I wasn't looking where I was going. This young man did all he could to avoid me. I feel so stupid," admitted Margaret, in spite of her innocence. The busboy rose to his feet with the tray loaded, confused by Margaret's actions.

"I'm quite willing to pay for whatever damage has been done here. My name is Margaret Olson. I'm with the party of forty in the function room." Margaret watched as the manager considered whether it made good business sense to charge the member of a two-thousand-dollar party for a few three-dollar plates and saucers? His answer came back no. The manager extended the busboy a lukewarm apology and wished Margaret a good evening. She walked into the ladies room with a smile on her face. If the busboy was going to lose his job, it wasn't going to be on her shift, she thought. However, something else had happened to Margaret. She did not believe in signs, or fate, and certainly not divine intervention. However, there was no arguing that this insignificant event had somehow altered her mindset. Instantaneously, her heart and her mind had been jolted into complete accord.

Returning to the function room, Margaret whispered into Reid's ear. She asked to speak to him in private. They returned to the gathering ten minutes later, but Margaret did not return to her chair. With Reid seated, she applied an affectionate squeeze to his shoulder and walked over to Claire.

"I'm heading over to Wells. Would you keep an eye on Reid for me? I just told him there was someone else. I'm sure he'll be fine but keep an eye on him anyway. Okay?" asked Margaret in an almost motherly fashion. Claire rose from her chair.

"Let me walk you to your car," she said. The two women left the hall and headed out across the busy main room. As they waited for the elevator to deliver them downstairs, Claire's tone grew serious.

"You're doing the right thing, Margaret. I want you to know that," counseled Claire. Margaret seemed confused by her friend's words. She stared directly into Claire's eyes, searching for the real meaning behind her statement.

"Reid's called me—at home. He's asked me to meet with him. Of course I haven't," explained Claire.

"When?" questioned an astonished Margaret.

"Over the last couple of weeks. Right after you two got back from vacation," she confessed. Margaret was too dumbfounded to reply. She leaned forward and hugged her friend, realizing what this must have been doing to her over the past two weeks.

Emerging from the parking lot, Margaret quickly steered her car onto Route 101 east and sped toward the coast. Just before reaching the interstate near Hampton it occurred to Margaret that she had neither a change of clothes nor toiletries of any kind. The lack of preparation or planning only served to heighten the excitement of the trip, however.

After passing through Portsmouth, the BMW sped up the Maine Turnpike to the Wells exit, where Margaret joined Route 1. While crawling south in traffic she noticed that the depression of recent weeks had lifted. The gloomy shroud that had attached itself to her in recent days was gone. The only matter that remained unresolved was whether Brian could be persuaded to take her back.

Margaret soon turned into the driveway of the Atlantic Coast Lodge. Seeing Brian's pickup truck in the corner of the overflow parking lot, her heart jumped. That meant he was here. Pulling into a vacant parking space by the door, it occurred to her that she had not even considered what she would say to him. She took a deep breath, stepped from the car, and climbed the stairs to the office. Millie, who was behind the front desk, appeared surprised, almost flustered, as Margaret entered the office.

"Hello, Millie. Would you tell Brian that I'd like to see him, please?" she asked respectfully.

"He's not here," came a curt reply. There was no one else in the lobby, allowing Millie the luxury of being borderline rude.

"His truck is right out in the yard," answered Margaret.

"He's not here," Millie repeated.

"Millie, I really have to see him. I'm not here to cause any trouble and I think he may actually want to hear what I have to say. I don't plan on leaving until I see him, so if you let him know I'm here it's going to make it easier on everyone concerned."

"He's out jogging, he's not here. If you head down Mile Road you'll probably spot him," said Millie, with only the hint of a thaw in her tone. Margaret thanked her and turned toward the door.

"You pull anything like you did a couple of months ago—well, I'll pay you a visit over in New Hampshire myself," Millie threatened, although she sounded less angry than before. Margaret nodded without turning and hopped back into the car.

Making the short drive to Mile Road, Margaret drove eastward through the grassy marshlands but there was no sign of Brian along her route. Pulling into the beach parking area, she found a spot by the ocean fence. From this point, Margaret could see approximately a mile in each direction. Hopping from the car, she stood against the fence and looked northward. There was no one between her and the jetty that even remotely resembled Brian. Running along the chain link fence, she looked south. Her eyes locked onto the tall, trim body of a jogger loping along the edge of the water. Margaret descended the stairs and took off after him. Seconds later, she removed one, then the other, of her flat-heeled shoes, tossing them onto the sand.

The beach was not very crowded as Margaret set out in full stride after the man she had removed from her life only two months earlier. The sun cast long shadows across the sand from the beachfront motels and guest houses. It was a prime time of the day to walk or jog along the coast. Margaret was gaining on an unsuspecting Brian as he leisurely plodded along the edge of the surf. She closed the gap between them to fifty, then forty, then thirty feet. The noise from the breaking waves to his left drowned out the sounds of her approach. The distance between them had shrunken to ten feet when she realized she had no idea what she would say to him. Acting on a spontaneous impulse, Margaret leaped from the sand and jumped high onto Brian's back, throwing her arms around his neck and locking her legs around his waist. Brian gave out an astonished gasp on impact and staggered forward.

"You proposed marriage to me back in June and I've decided to accept," Margaret called out.

"What the hell is going on?" shouted Brian, his mind working feverishly to sort out what was happening to him. "Who the hell are you?" he asked, although by now aware of whom was riding his back.

"Who am I? You asked me to marry you back in June!" she cried out.

"I asked a lot of women to marry me in June! Which one are you?" he asked. Margaret was encouraged that Brian would joke with her.

"It's Maggie," she blurted out. Brian did not respond. Instead he stared straight ahead in silence.

"I'm warning you, Kelly. I have a battery of lawyers back in New Hampshire waiting to sue your ass off for alienation of affection if you try backing out on me," Margaret threatened.

"You're suing me for alienation of affection?" he asked in disbelief. "What about the letter?"

"You never opened it. You just threw it in my face. For all you know it was an acceptance," she answered.

"You—are—unbelievable! Only you would have the fucking nerve to pull something like this." Brian had turned serious.

"Are you saying you don't love me anymore?" asked Margaret. Brian did not answer for a few moments.

"No, I truthfully can't say that," he said, almost regretfully.

"Then forgive me—and say you'll take me back," she pleaded.

"And how do I know you won't pull this same shit again?"

"Because now I know what it's like to try getting over you, and I don't want to ever have to go through this again. Brian, I love you. You're in my blood, dammit!" Margaret began to cry as Brian resumed walking down the beach. He was still carrying her. A couple, clearly tourists, passed by and attempted not to stare. Brian walked for a full minute before coming to a halt.

"You will have to make some concessions," he stated firmly.

"Like what?" Margaret asked.

"For starters, I hate this hyphen crap with names. I want you to be Maggie Kelly—not Maggie Keogh-Olson-Kelly. Maggie Kelly!"

"Margaret Kelly sounds like a cleaning woman's name," she said, pretending to be insulted.

"Maggie, it doesn't sound like you're very serious—"

"Okay, agreed—no hyphens. It's Margaret Kelly." Brian turned back to her and smiled.

"Is there anything else?" Margaret asked impatiently.

"I think we ought to have at least one child together. I'm absolutely serious," said Brian.

"I agree," blurted out Margaret. "I've been thinking about having more children, too."

Brian was pleasantly surprised.

"That stuff I said back in June about signing a prenuptial agreement, that's off the table now. If you pull any of this shit after we're married, then I'll pick you clean in divorce court."

Margaret laughed aloud and consented by a whisper into his ear.

"I want us married in a church, maybe a Catholic church. In any event, I want a priest there for the ceremony."

"When did you suddenly turn religious?" she roared. "You know I'm not very religious, Brian. Why are you making this so difficult?"

"I've had a lot of time to think lately—thanks mostly to you. My life is this directionless mess and I've decided to turn it around. Now, if this is too much to ask from you...."

"Agreed, but that had better be the last of this concession shit," threatened Margaret.

"Oh, and I think we should live in my house here and not over in Bedford," stated Brian tentatively.

Margaret pushed her locked heels against his crotch, causing him to call out. "Maybe I'll just withdraw that last demand. Perhaps I was getting a little greedy with that one?" he admitted good-naturedly. With that said, Margaret jumped down and kissed him for the first time in months. They held each other for over a minute before stepping back.

"Brian, you're going to have to help me out. I don't have a change of clothes, or any toiletries, or any place to stay," she said pathetically.

"Where are your shoes, Maggie May?"

"Oh, and I may not have any shoes either. I left them by the stairs to the parking lot."

"It sounds like I'm going to get stuck putting you up for the weekend, Keogh," he said in mock disgust. "Well, Maggie May, that means putting my religious thing on hold for at least a couple of more days anyway," he complained. Margaret looked up at Brian, tears still welling up in her eyes.

"You're calling me Maggie May again. I can't believe I'm back here," she muttered warmly, as she wrapped her arms around him. "You knew. You always knew."

Brian stared down on her warmly. "I guess I really did, but you had me going pretty good this summer," he confessed.

"Oh, getting back to putting me up this weekend, remember that thing you started telling me about last June? You know, the thing that drove one woman in ten raving mad?" Margaret asked, with a devilish expression.

"Let's find your shoes first," Brian smiled.

Epilogue

Margaret and Brian were married in a Roman Catholic ceremony in Bedford, New Hampshire, in November 1992. On December 15, 1993, they were blessed with a daughter.

In September 1995, Claire Gagnon became engaged to James Doucette, a man seven years her junior whom she had met through his employment with Margaret Kelly & Associates, Certified Public Accountants.

About the Author

Tom Coughlin is a certified public account who also has a back-ground as a corporate internal auditor, teacher and radio announcer. He received his undergraduate and graduate degrees from New Hampshire College where he is an adjunct faculty member. He has taught at Rivier and Hesser colleges, also in New Hampshire.

A resident of New Hampshire for more than thirty years, Tom and his wife, Elaine, and their family live in the town of Chester, a rustic, New England community twelve miles from his Manchester office. He wrote much of *Maggie May's Diary,* his first novel, at the family's cliff-side summer cottage on Great Wass Island, off the eastern tip of Maine. Great Wass Island was the setting for Stephen King's novel, *Dolores Claiborne.*